Coaching The English Premier League 4-4-2

by

David Williams

Published by
WORLD CLASS COACHING

First published January, 2003 by
WORLD CLASS COACHING 9205 W. 131 Terr, Overland Park, KS 66213 (913) 402-0030

ISBN 0-9718218-7-9

Author - David Williams
Edited by Mike Saif

Front Cover - Ashley Cole of Arsenal challenges David Beckham of Manchester United during an English Premier League game.

WORLD CLASS COACHING would like to thank
worldofsoccer.com for the use of the graphics

Published by
WORLD CLASS COACHING

FOREWORD

To be successful in any team game, organization is vital. Even the world's greatest players need to be part of a system that allows them to express themselves. For some coaches the 4 - 4 - 2 formation will be seen simply as the positions players take up on the field. This book goes beyond the team simply having a shape on the field and considers the roles and responsibilities of each player when attacking and defending.

David Williams is somebody I've known for many years, I chose him as my first team coach during the latter stages of my time as manager of Leeds United. He has played and coached at all levels of the game and draws on his experience to inform the reader of how the 4 - 4 - 2 formation can be implemented and how it varies between the top English Premier League clubs.

For many years the 4 - 4 - 2 has been the preferred system of playing in England. Practically all the recent English Premier League Champions play with a 4 - 4 - 2 formation causing other teams to follow.

Coaches from various backgrounds, working at all levels, will find this book an interesting read. There will be ideas they agree with and opinions they go against, which make for the ingredients of a thought provoking book.

David Williams has done an excellent job explaining the 4 - 4 - 2 formation and I'm sure coaches of all levels will benefit enormously from this book.

Howard Wilkinson

Coaching The English Premier League 4-4-2

01 Opposing Player

X1 4-4-2 Player

Path of Player

Path of Ball

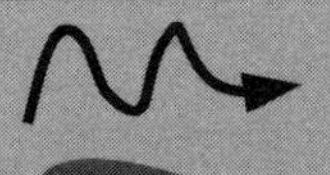

Path of Dribble

Target Area

Introduction

Soccer pundits, as well as enthusiastic supporters, always get a thrill out of discussing the 'system' that teams play. The problem with this, is that they often think that the system is everything and is the road to success.

Unfortunately, its not as simple as that. The system cannot be ignored, but the coach has to look at his players and play to their strengths. He has to ensure that his team understand the system he feels suits them best.

Having done this, he is then in their hands. Once the players step on the field, they are the ones who make the system succeed or fail.

In England, of the many systems available, the 4-4-2 is the most popular. Manchester United, Arsenal and Liverpool, the three top teams in the English Premier League, all use this style, although as this book will show, all slightly differently.

This book sets out to try and demonstrate a progression of practices to help the reader understand how this shape may be employed in both attacking and defending situations. Many of the principles used are soccer principles and would apply whatever system was employed. However, the step by step progression will, I hope, give even inexperienced coaches the confidence to go ahead and use the 4-4-2 formation with their own players in an effective way.

So why the 4-4-2 and what are the strengths of this system?

First, it offers a good balance, it 'fills' the field giving the team width and depth. Next, there are units which the coach can work on and which can inspire team spirit. For example, the back four wanting to keep a clean sheet (shutout).

It also encourages players to work in pairs in areas of the field. This engenders good team play, where for example, the right back and the wide right midfield players will want to win the 'battle' on their flank. Similarly, the two central midfield players will want to dominate their direct opponents.

Chapter One

Defending With The Back Four

To start with, all defending relies on the individual and his ability to know when and how to tackle, to intercept, to delay and not to get beaten. If the player isn't a good individual defender, he will have difficulty no matter what the formation is.

Beyond defending individually, the player needs to understand his role in the team's defending - when and how to mark and when to cover and fill space.

These are the aspects of defending we shall look at, defending as part of a unit. The smallest of these is two players working together. The first, directly challenging the player in possession and his partner adopting a covering, support position.

In the first practice, X1 and X2 defend against O1 and O2. X1 plays the ball across and follows quickly to close down the space and prevent the receiver moving towards the end/target line. X1 should move quickly, watch the receiver's control in case a bad first touch allows a tackle.

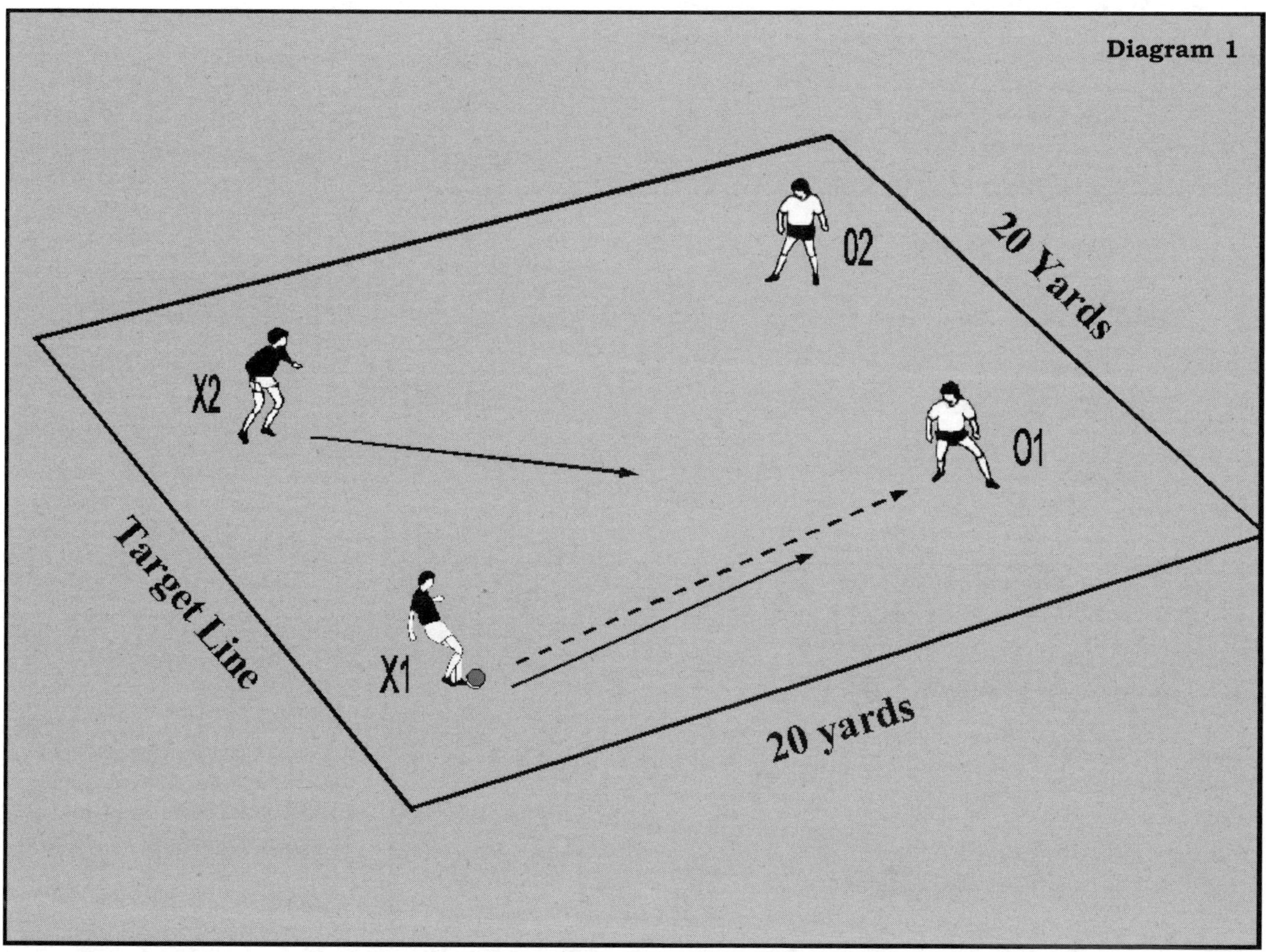

X1 plays the ball to O1 and then follows his pass to defend. X2 takes up a covering position.

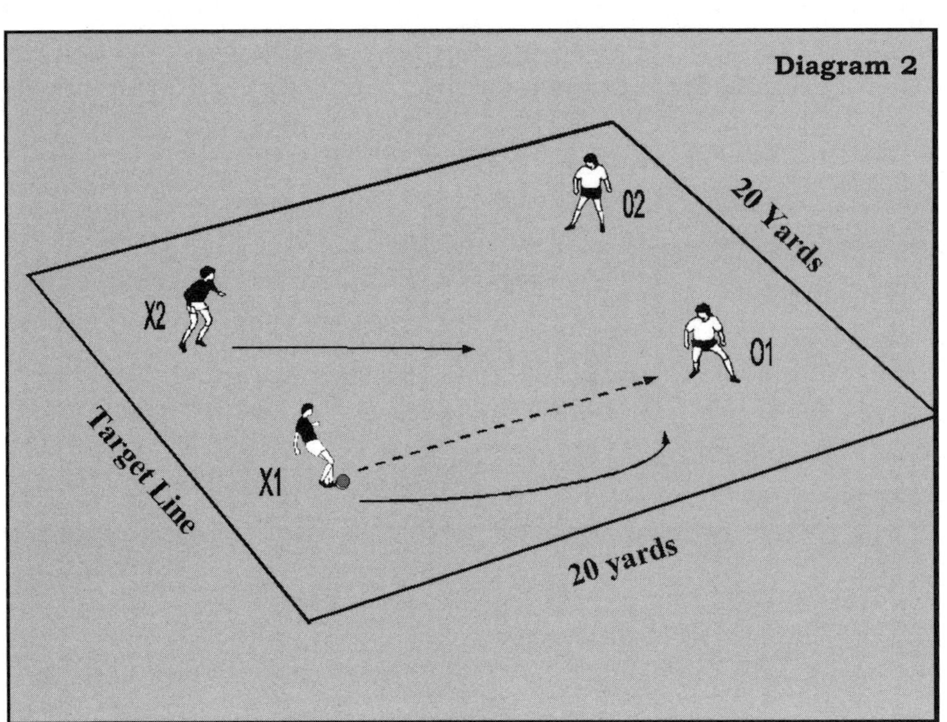

X1 should try to angle his approach so that O1 is encouraged to move inside towards X2.

X1 needs to get close enough to 01 so that O1 has to look down at the ball.

If X1 is able to turn O1 back towards his own line, then he should move in quickly, maintain the pressure, and keep forcing him back.

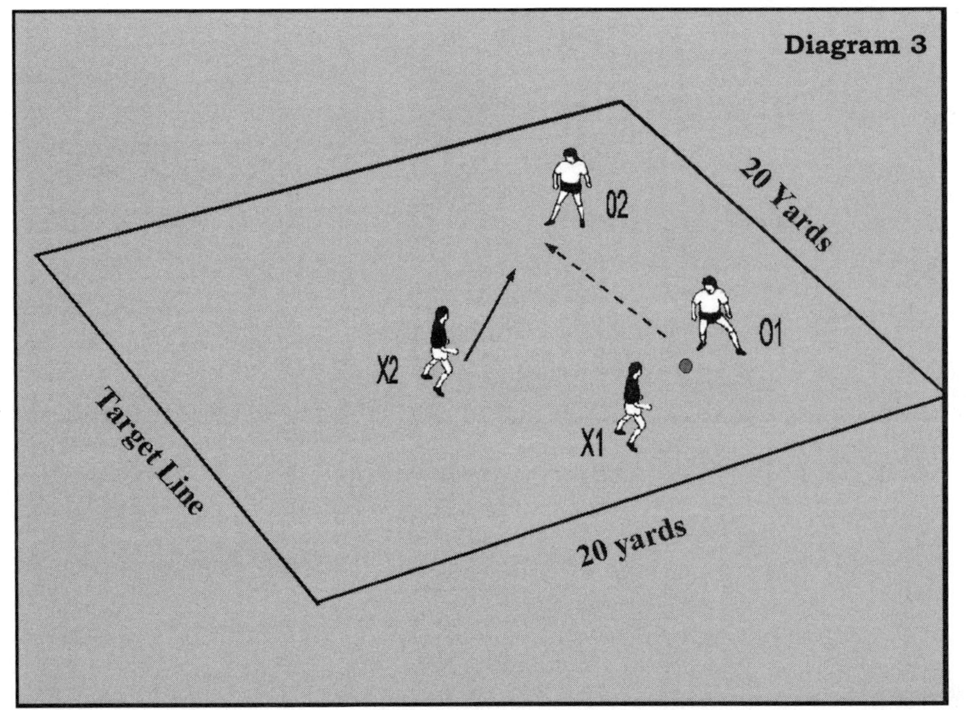

X2 also moves quickly and looks to position himself in a covering position. His covering position is as shown, behind and inside X1.

X2 needs to be able to see O2 and, should a pass to O2 be made, be ready to move quickly to intercept, tackle O2 or snap up a poor touch.

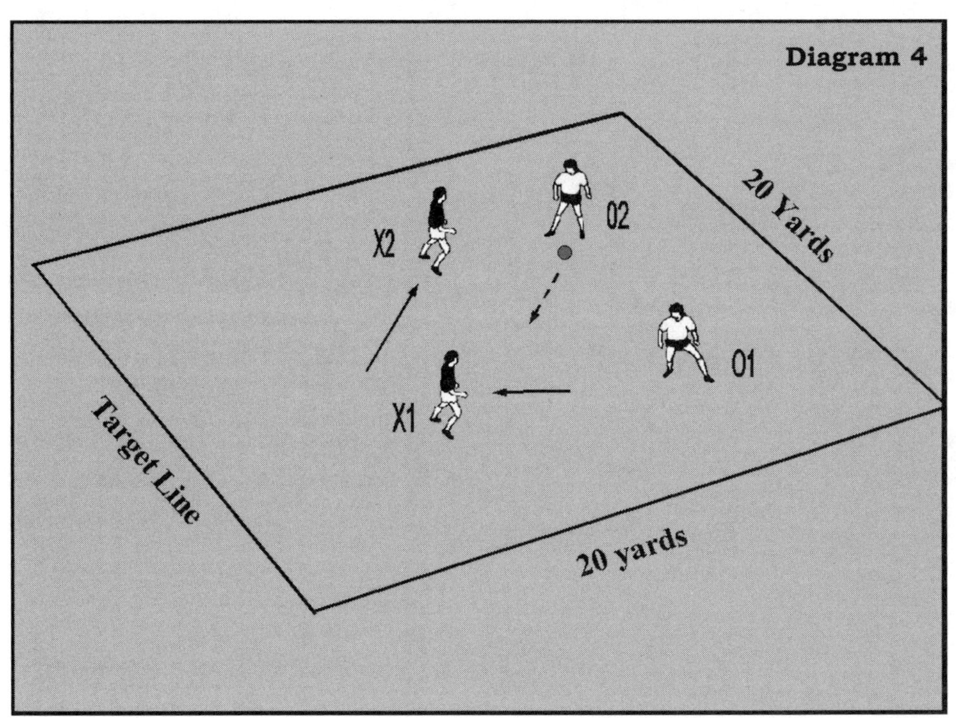

If X2 isn't able to intercept or steal the ball, he should position himself so that O2 is encouraged to move inside rather than outside.

In doing this, X1 should have then taken up the covering position.

The practice can be developed so that X's and O's take turns at defending and attacking.

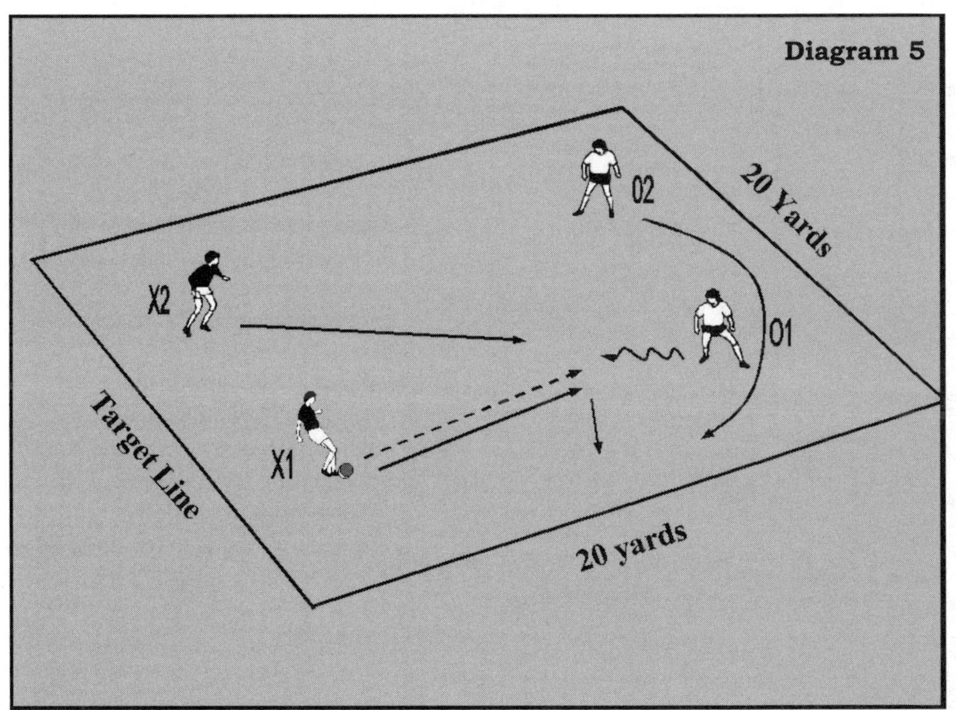

One movement which needs addressing is how the defenders cope if O1 and O2 cross over.

Correct

If O2 makes a run/overlap behind O1, the correct movements for the defenders are as shown - X1 backs off to track the run of O2, X2 closes in on O1.

The result is, X2 confronting O1 and forcing him towards X1, the covering defender.

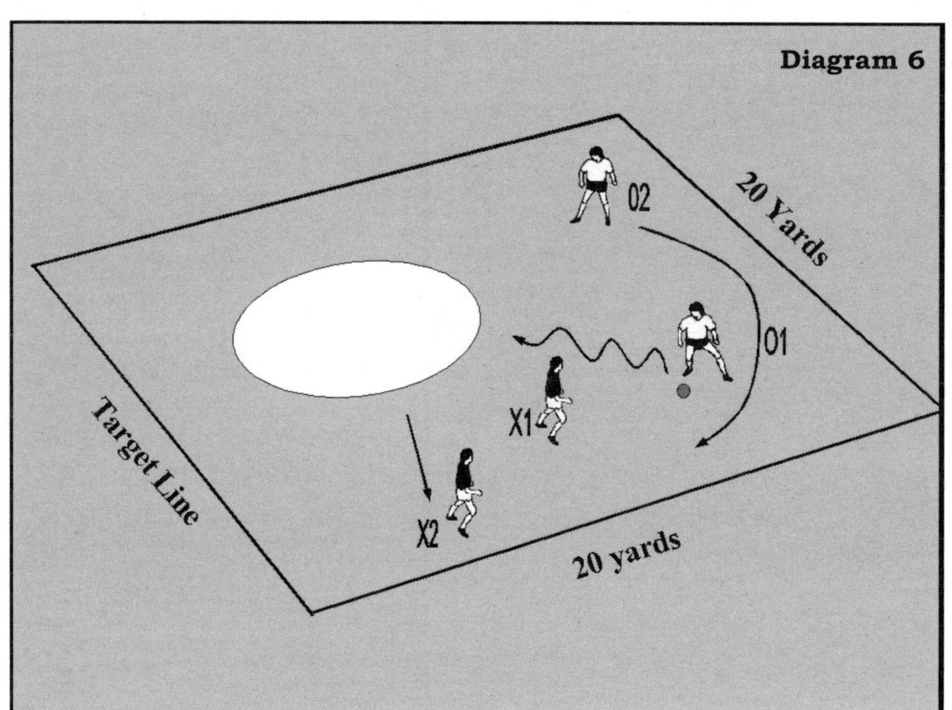

Incorrect

The mistake often made is for X2 to react by running directly behind X1 to track O2, leaving O1 with a clear space to run into vacated by X2.

cp: close down quickly, covering defender should be able to see player he's marking and the ball.

The area is now made longer (30 yards). The same principles apply as in the previous exercises

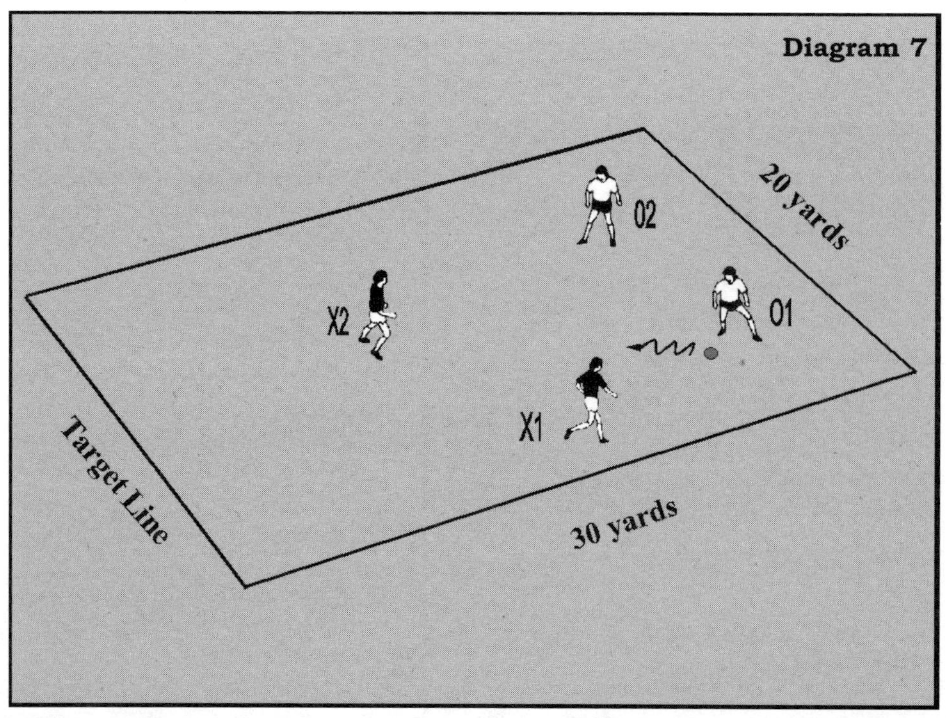

In order to cope with this added distance (space), the defender needs to understand how to slow the forward down. This is done initially by reducing the distance between defender and forward as much as possible and then the defender being able to back off, 'jockey', in a well balanced and controlled way, while at the same time guiding the forward inside towards his partner.

The principles established so far are expanded into the beginnings of work with the back four. This practice is designed simply to get the four defenders to understand how they need to react to the movement of the ball and the movement of forwards.

It's a passive practice where the four forwards move the ball and make the defenders adjust their positions. The forwards can dribble at the defenders without intending to beat them and the covering players have to understand their responsibilities. The coach needs to make sure that each player fully understands the distance he needs to be from the player when challenging for the ball, the other defenders and the man he is marking.

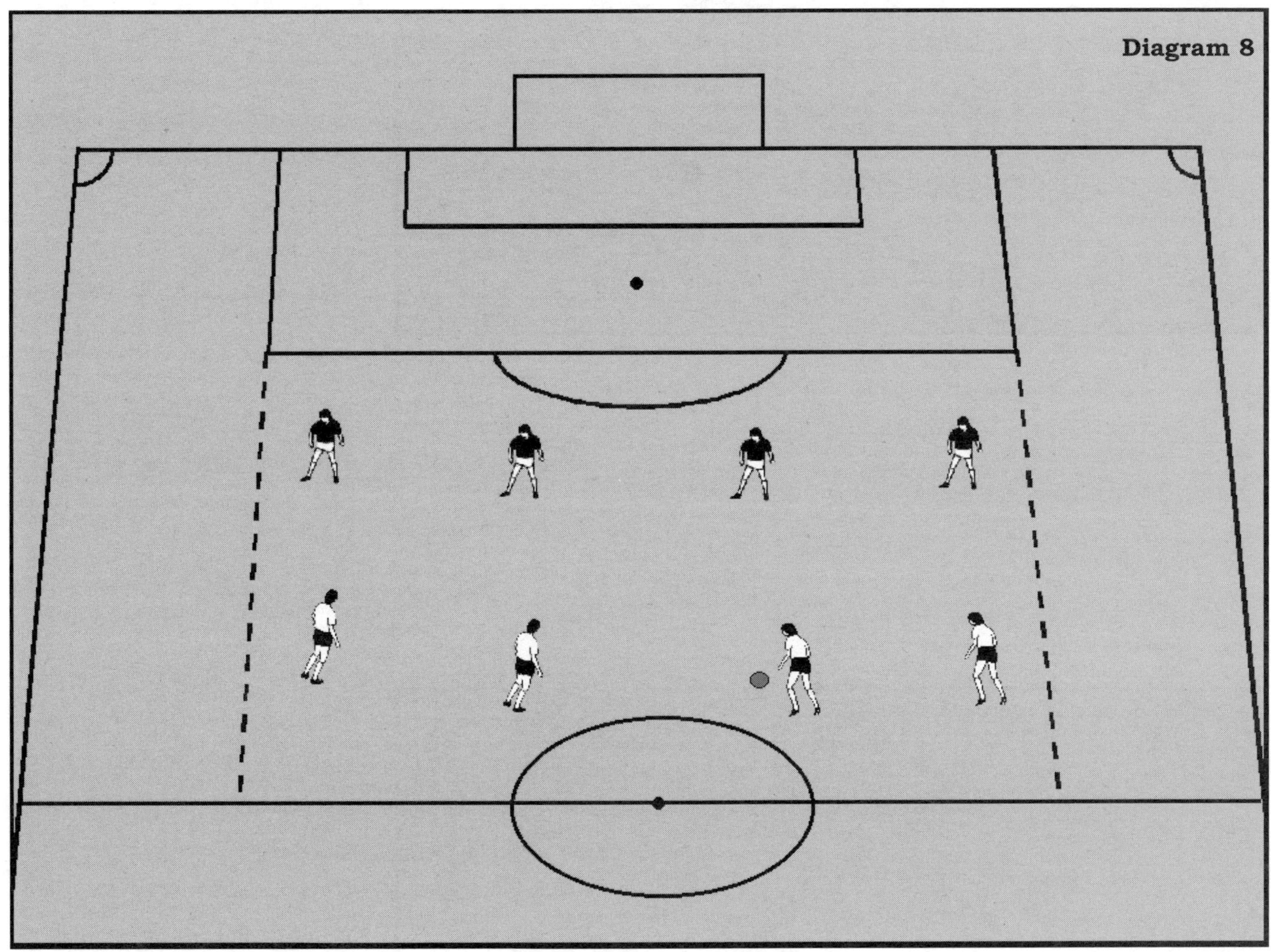

This is the initial set up for the practice. The area is between the half-line and lines extending from both sides of the penalty area. As the ball is moved from forward to forward, the defenders move accordingly. Each player has to position himself according to the ball and the forward he is marking.

NB: The Attackers can dribble Forward then come back

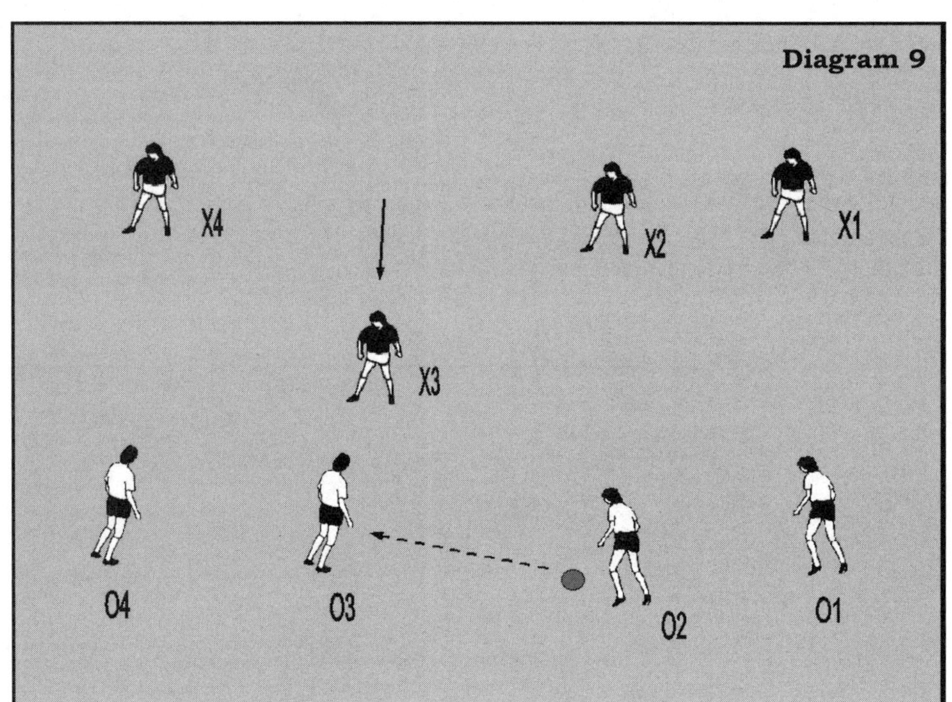

If the ball is passed to O3, X3 should step and pressure the ball.

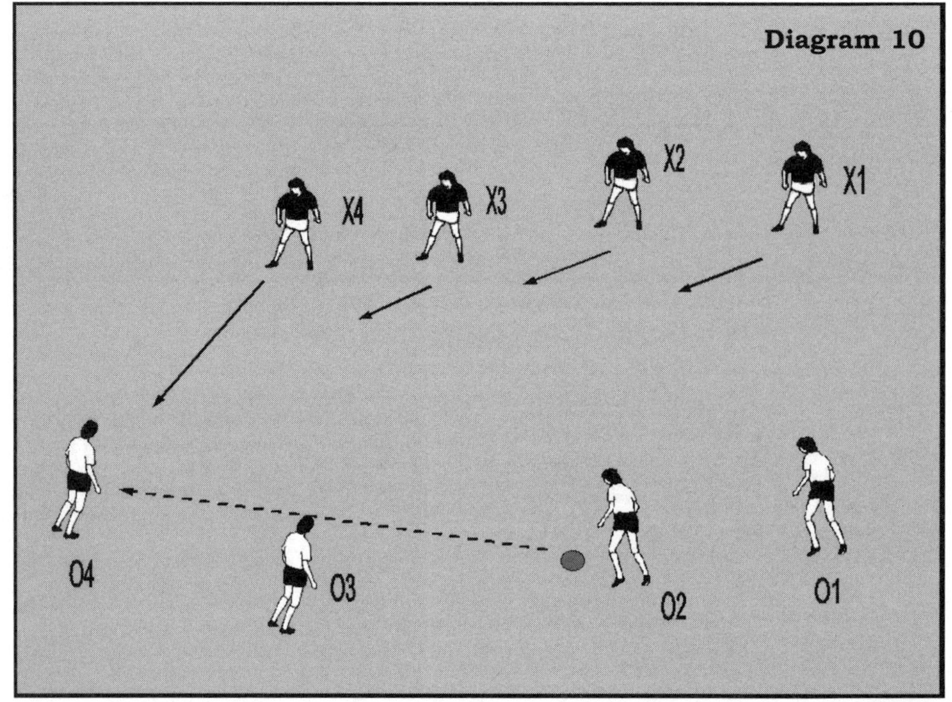

If the ball is passed out wide to O4, X4 should pressure the ball and the other three defenders should slide over to that side of the field.

X4 should try and position himself so he forces O4 inside toward X3.

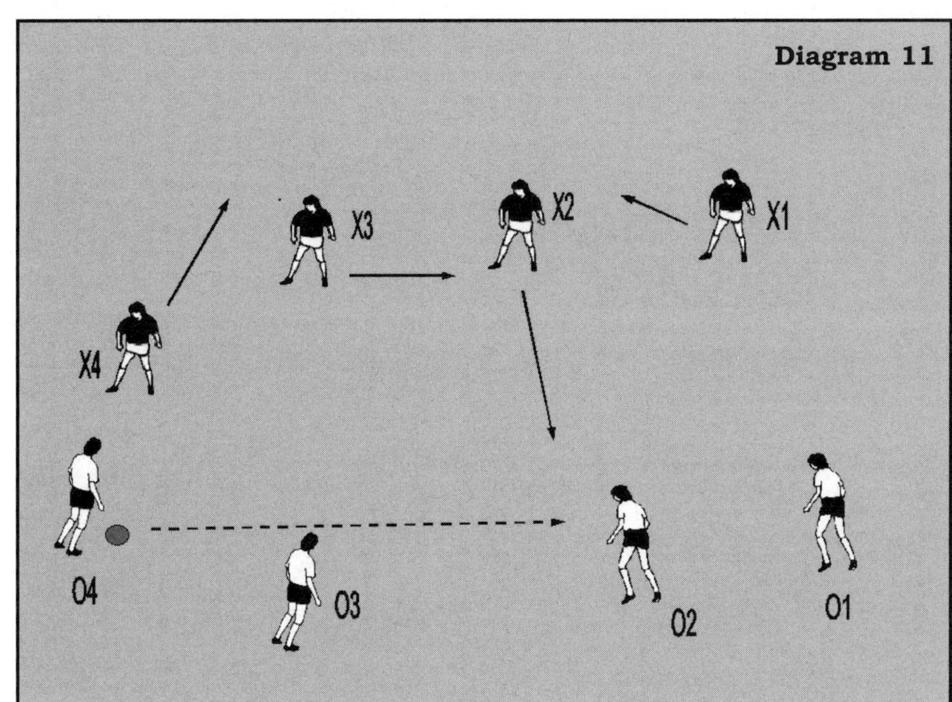

If the ball is passed inside to O2, X2 moves quickly to pressure O2, while X4, X3 and X1 adjust their positions.

X3 and X1 give immediate cover and X4 takes up a position to balance the defense by being the furthest player away.

X2, in pressuring O2 shouldn't go straight at him but be angled and has a choice of forcing him toward X1 or X3.

c/: Move side to side as unit; force wide players inside; supporting defenders should cover deep vs press up on the man they're marking.

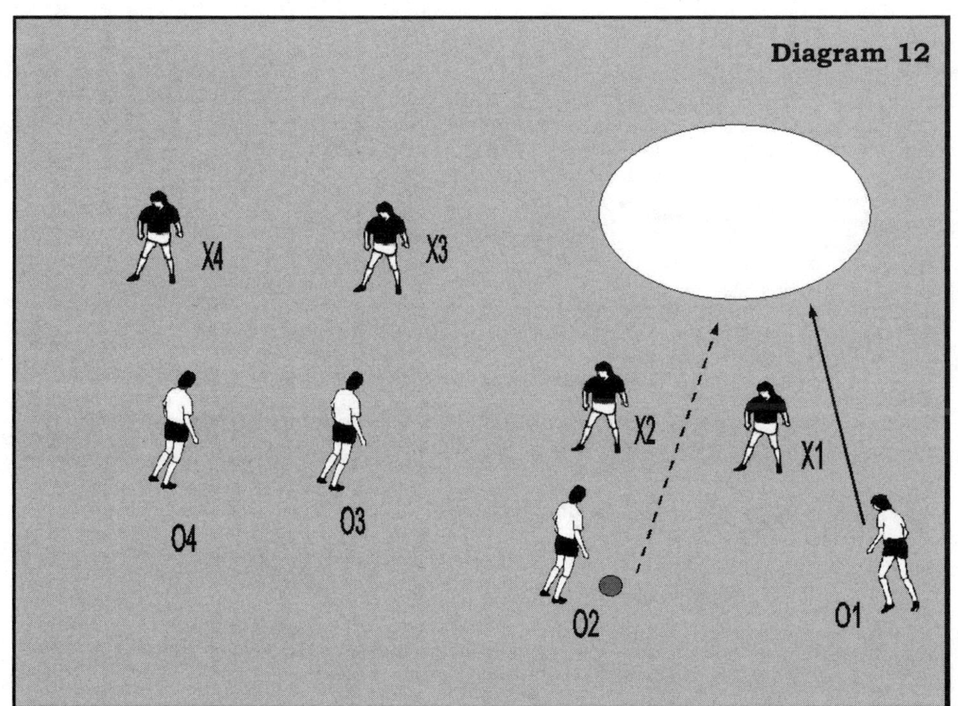

Incorrect
In this example, X1 is in a poor position. He is pushed up too far on O1, leaving space behind him that could be exploited by a through-ball.

Use a full half pitch and now include a goalkeeper. The back four set themselves 10-15 yards outside the penalty area. The attacking players are in four lines, numbered clearly 1 through 4 and spread across the width of the field. Each line has a supply of balls with the front players always having a ball ready at their feet. The coach calls a number, e.g. 2, this means that the front player from line 2 is the player who starts the attack with his ball. He is joined by the front player from lines 1,3 and 4 without a ball.

The practice is therefore designed to make the back four react quickly and accurately to wherever the threat comes.

4 v 4 is now played until a goal is scored, a shot is saved, the ball gets out of play or the back four win possession.

If the back four win possession, it is a good idea to give them a target e.g. chip a pass to one of the lines, or find the coach with a pass.

All the principles that have been mentioned before are now highlighted in a more realistic practice.

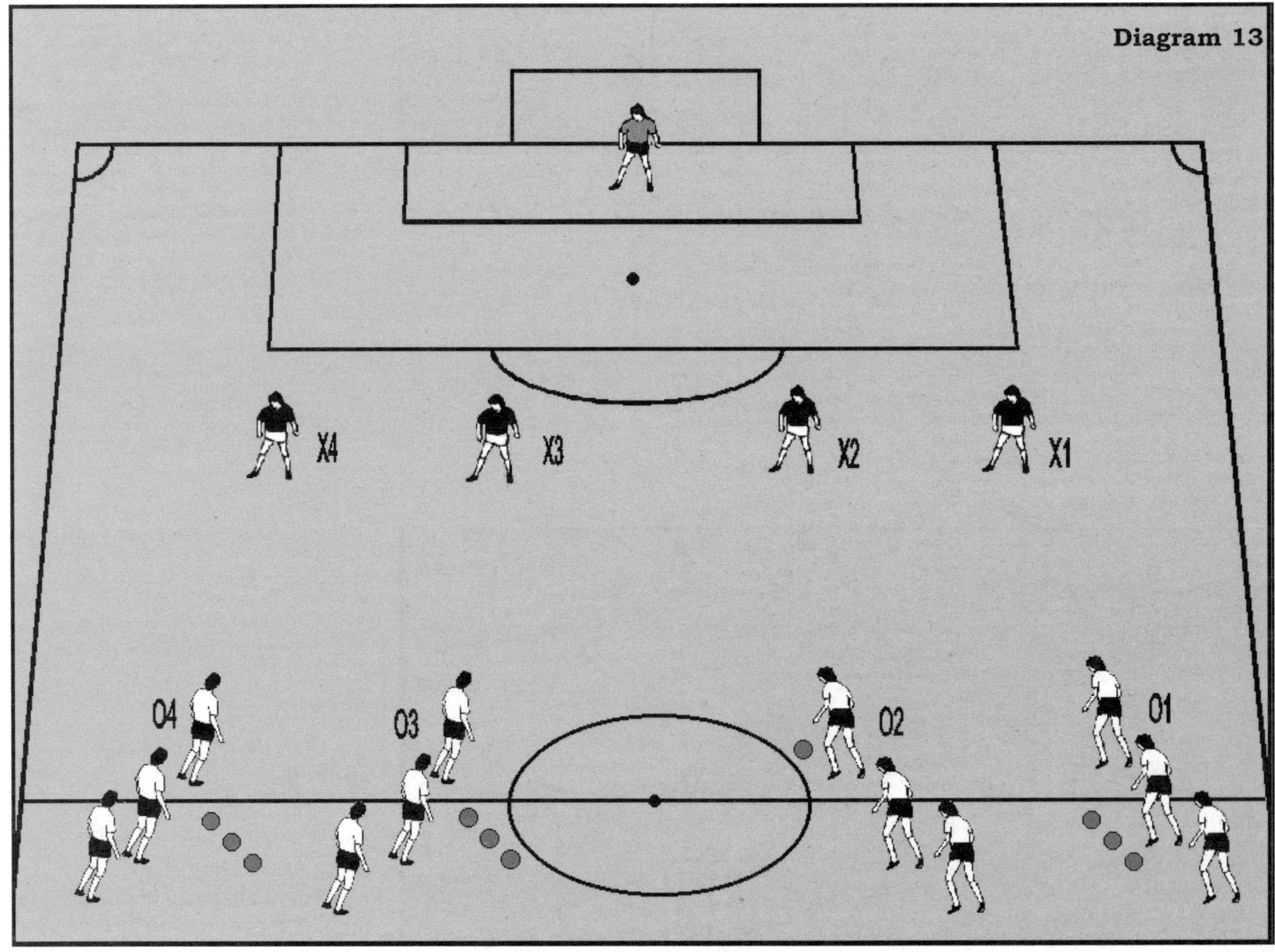

Back 4 start 1/2 between midfield an PK box.

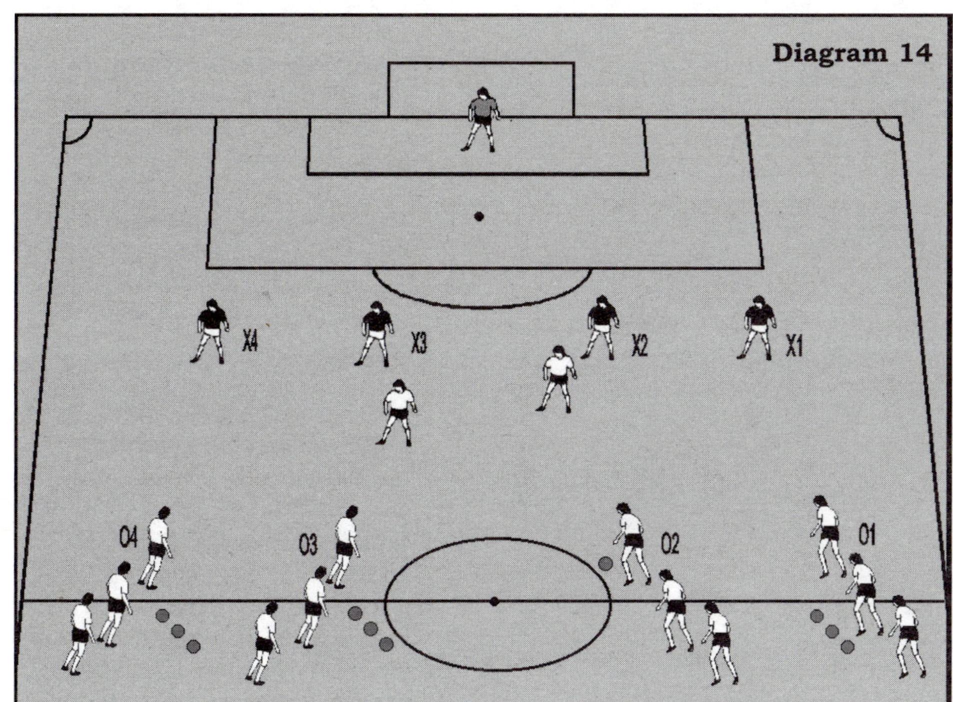

Diagram 14

This exercise is set up in the same way as the previous practice, with one addition. Two forwards are added to the attack to overload it 6 v 4 or 5 if the goalkeeper is included.

Including the forwards means that the attack now has some depth and players from lines 2 and 3 act more like midfield players.

Depth is important because there are times when the ball is passed backwards and the back four should realize that this is an opportunity to step forward. Not 'race' forward but move away from their own goal in a controlled way.

> Tell wingers they can move up but Line O2 & O3 to hold back as CM's - this encourages back passes & can coach refusal to move up.
> encourage them to play into strikers

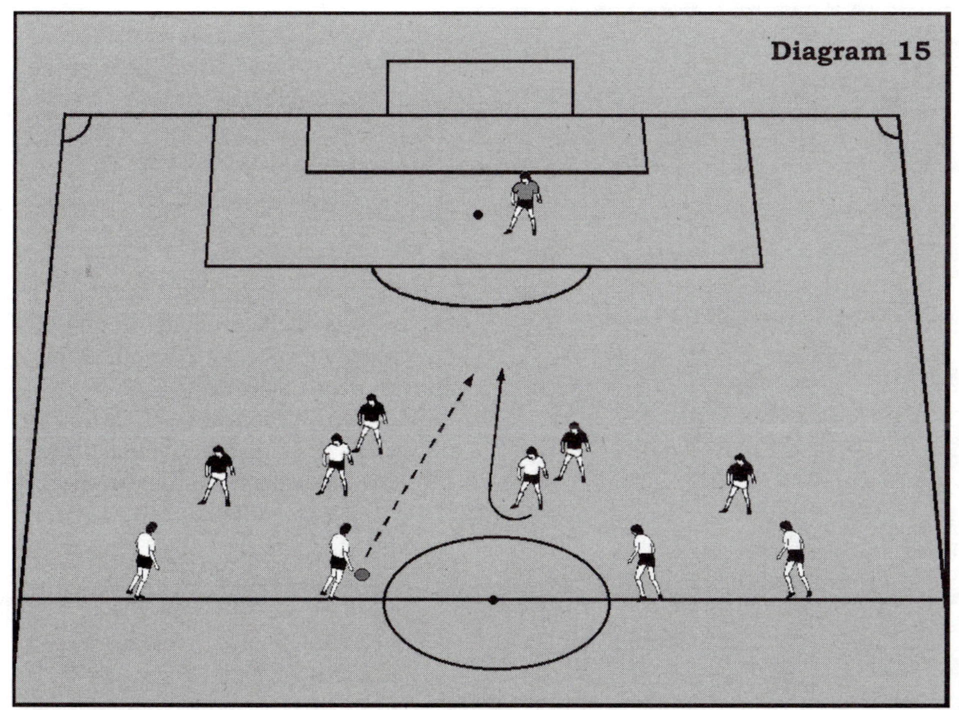

Diagram 15

The distance from the goal and the goalkeeper need to be explained.

If the back four drop too deep, they encourage shots. If they push too far up the field, as shown, they can be exploited by a through-pass in the space behind them which the goalkeeper can't get to it.

The goalkeeper also has a role to play. If he is too far back near his goal line, he won't be in a position to reach and clear any through balls. However, if he is too far out of his goal, he could get beaten by a long-range shot over his head.

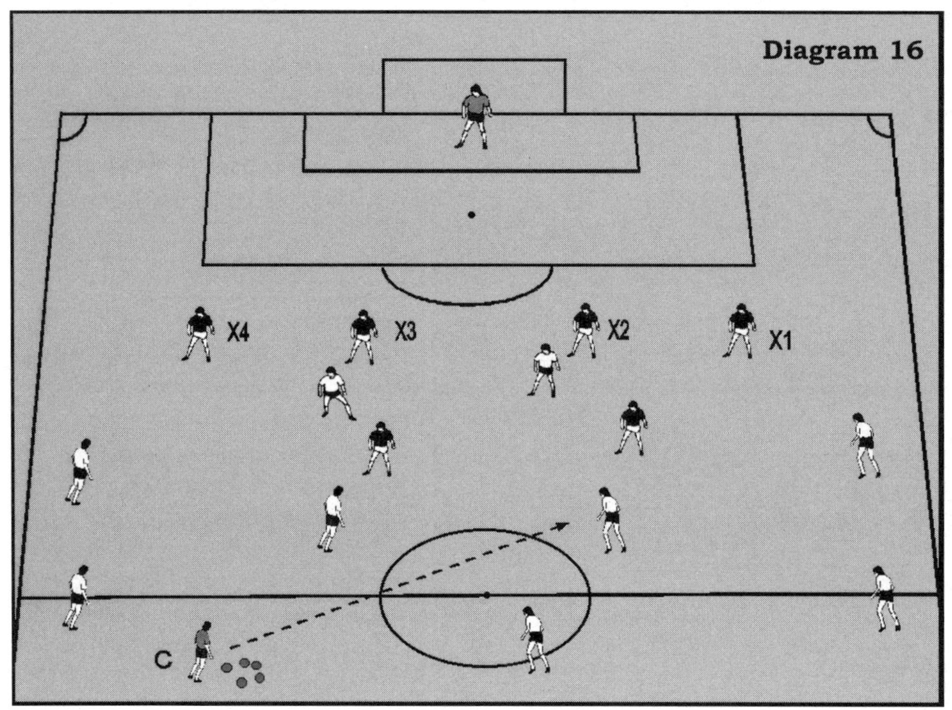

This is a functional practice with an overload against the back four and the introduction of two midfield players to assist in the defending.

The coach controls the start of the practice by playing balls to any of the attacking players. The defenders must then quickly organize their shape.

As far as the back four are concerned, all points previously made should now be reinforced.

With younger or inexperienced players it can often be a good time to call "STOP" and just look at each defender in turn to make sure they know their responsibility and that they are in the correct position.

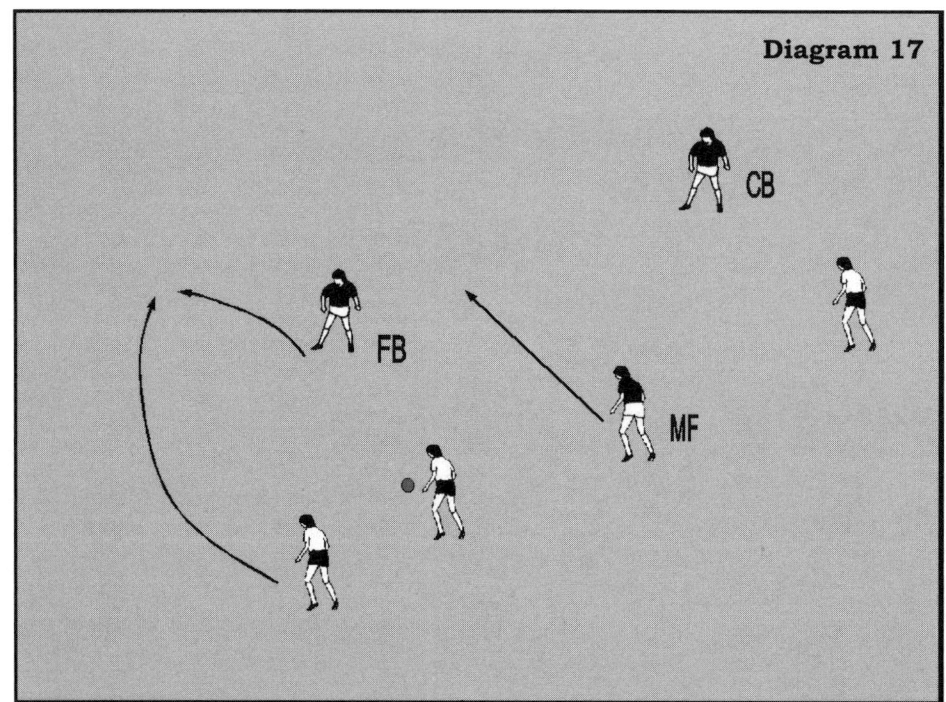

An area of concern is on the flanks, where the fullbacks can be exposed in 2 v 1 situations.

This situation needs to be recognized quickly by the FB, and also by the supporting defenders.

Ideally the player that helps the FB is the midfielder. If the MF player can provide support, then the back four remains intact.

In this situation the FB attempts to slow down the forward movement of the player with the ball. This gives time for the MF to get back and help. Then, as in earlier practices, the FB covers the overlapping player and the MF pressures the ball.

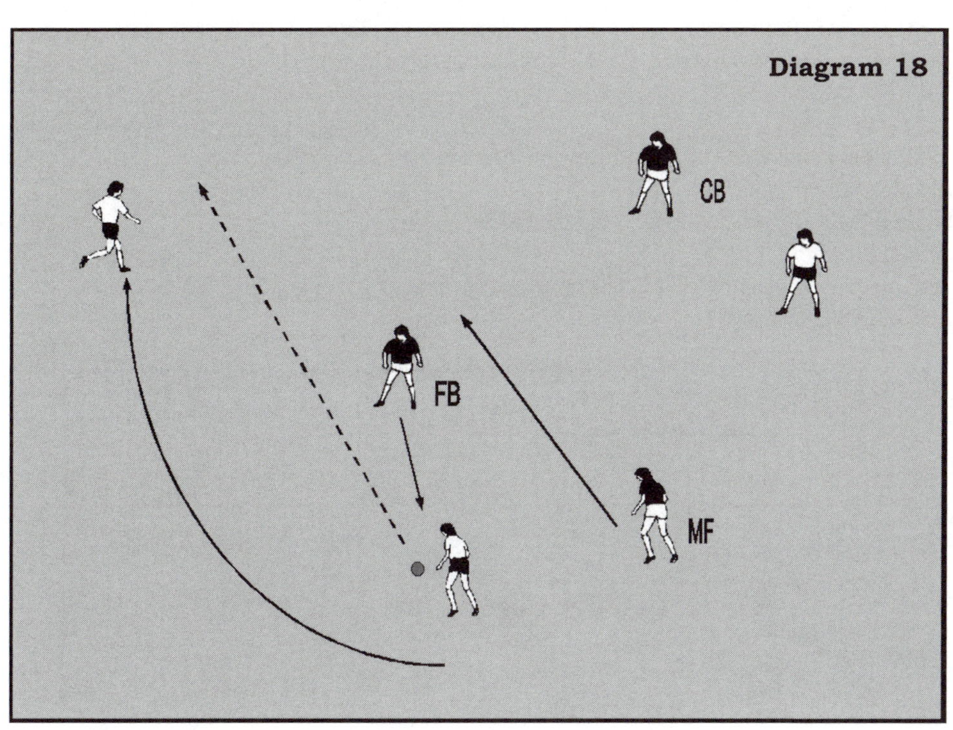

Incorrect

If the FB pressures the ball, this leaves the overlapping player free to make his run and receive the ball.

This situation makes it practically impossible for the MF or CB make a recovery run and be able to pressure the overlapping player once he has received the ball.

cp: Full back tracks overlapping player, ideally MF slides over to engage player [illegible] in possesion, if not the CB must & if he does the other Defenders must slide over

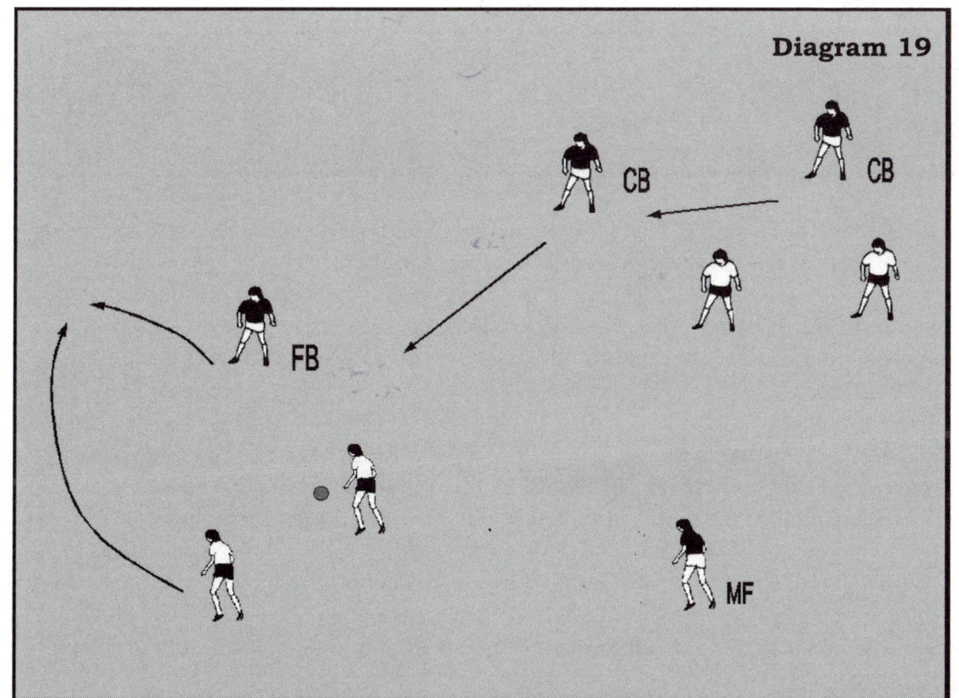

If the midfielder isn't in a position to run back and help the FB, then the inside CB needs to be ready to move across. This should produce a chain reaction where the other CB and FB also adjust.

Very often the back four can be described as being 'joined together' by an imaginary rope. Thus the movement of one of the four defenders causes the movement of the other three.

What is vital is that the fullback does not allow the overlapping player to go free. Such an action turns the whole team and causes confusion. It is impossible in this situation for any defender to adequately cover this run and prevent a cross going into the box.

One situation that often occurs and can cause confusion for the defenders, is when the opposing team's fullbacks have the ball. It is worthwhile for the coach to walk through this situation. O3 has the ball in this situation.

X1 should be getting tight to O11,
X2 is marking O9 'touch line side' or 'ball side' and is ready to cover the space behind X1 (space A).
X3 marks 'ball side' of O10 and is ready to cover space B.
X4 marks the 'ball side' of O7, the least dangerous forward, and covers space C.
X8 should try to get in a position to stop a pass from 03 to 09.
X6 needs to be in a position to see 06 and also cover space D. This is important because if X8 "goes to sleep" and ball watches, 08 may make a forward run behind X8. X6 needs to cover this.

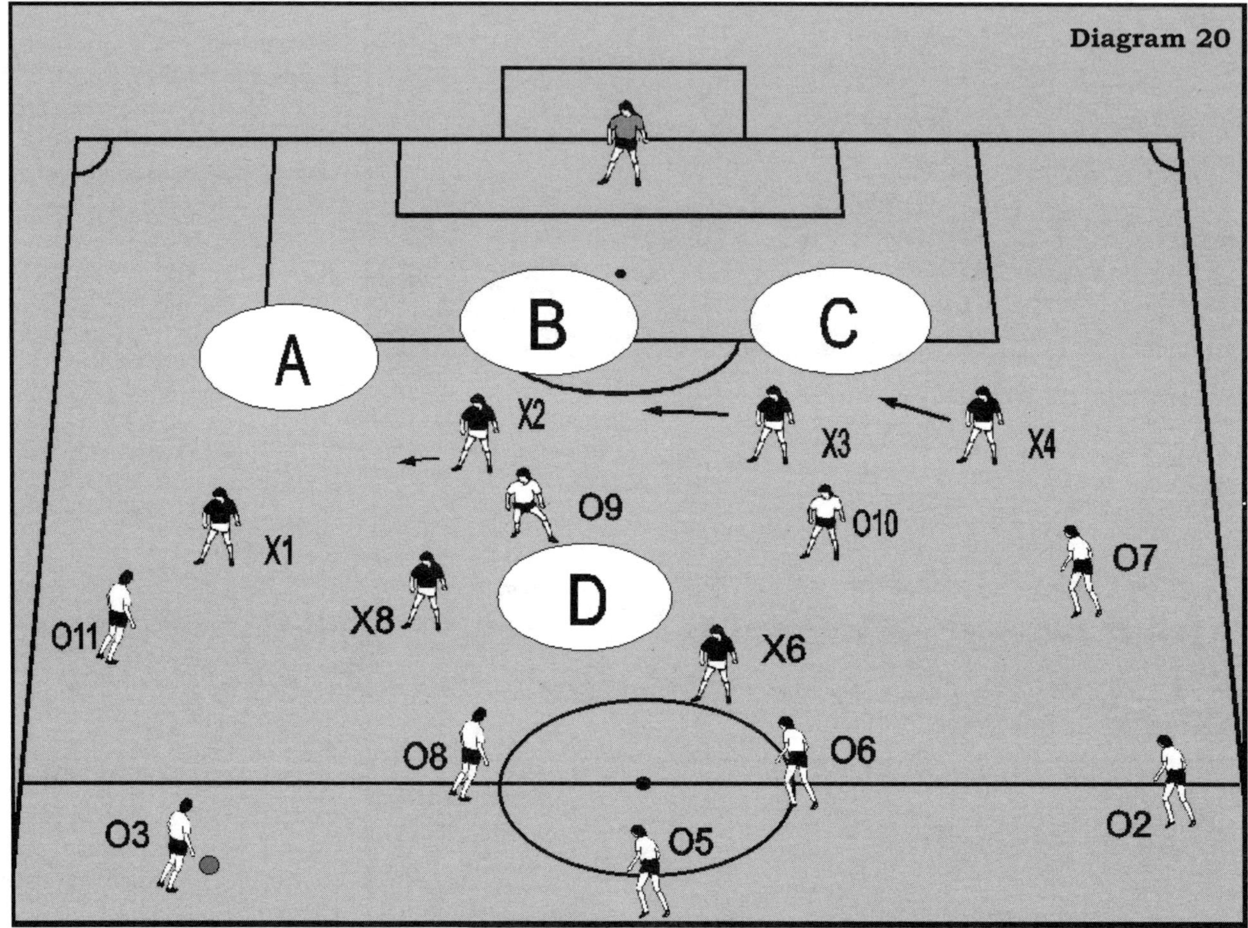

The shape of the back line is also crucial. X2 sets the line, but should not try to play offside. His rule for setting the line is simply, can he be first to the ball played into space A and get there before any of the forwards?

If a forward makes a 'bad' run behind the line of the defenders (X2, X3 and X4) into this space before the ball is played, X2 may leave him to be offside. However, communication is critical for the defenders and X2 should only leave the forward to run offside provided he gets a shout from X3.

X3 needs to position himself so that he can be first to a ball in space B. Again, if a forward makes a bad run into space B, X3 should easily be able to leave this player offside because he can see X2 and he should know that X4 should be positioning himself level with the other defenders in the back line and therefore will never be deeper than himself.

X4 concerns himself with space C and should never be deeper than X2 and X3 since he cannot cover space A or space B.

Of course when the ball is with O2 all the positions are reversed but the coach should walk through this as well.

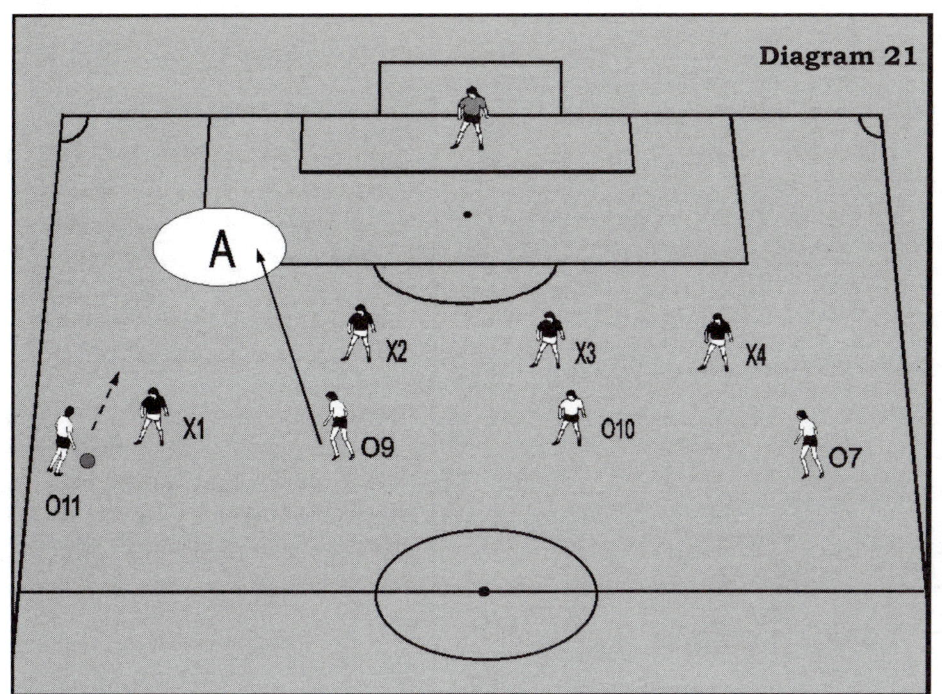

Diagram 21

If O9 makes a "bad" run into space A, BEFORE O11 passes the ball, X2 has the option to maintain his position and allow O9 to run past him as O9 will be in an offside position when the ball is passed to him.

In this example, X3 and X4 are in the correct position by staying level (flat) with X2.

Remember, it is critical that X2, X3 and X4 all communicate, hold their line and understand that it is okay to allow O9 to run past them as long as he does so before the ball is passed by O11.

NB: This was shown with defenders on line 1/2 way between midfield and top of penalty box.

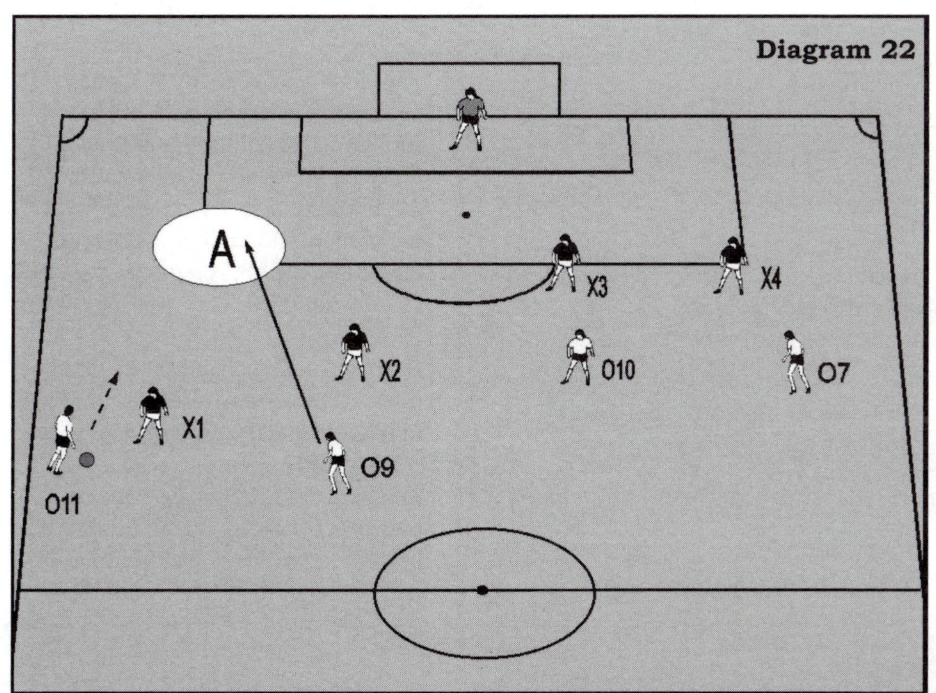

Diagram 22

In this example, X3 and X4 are not in a good position as they are deeper than X2. Therefore, O9 can run behind X2 before the ball is passed and still be in an onside position.

As stated earlier, it is critical that all the defenders are on the same page. Even if just one defender (X3 OR X4) drops deep, it makes it impossible for X2 to mark O9 AND space A behind him.

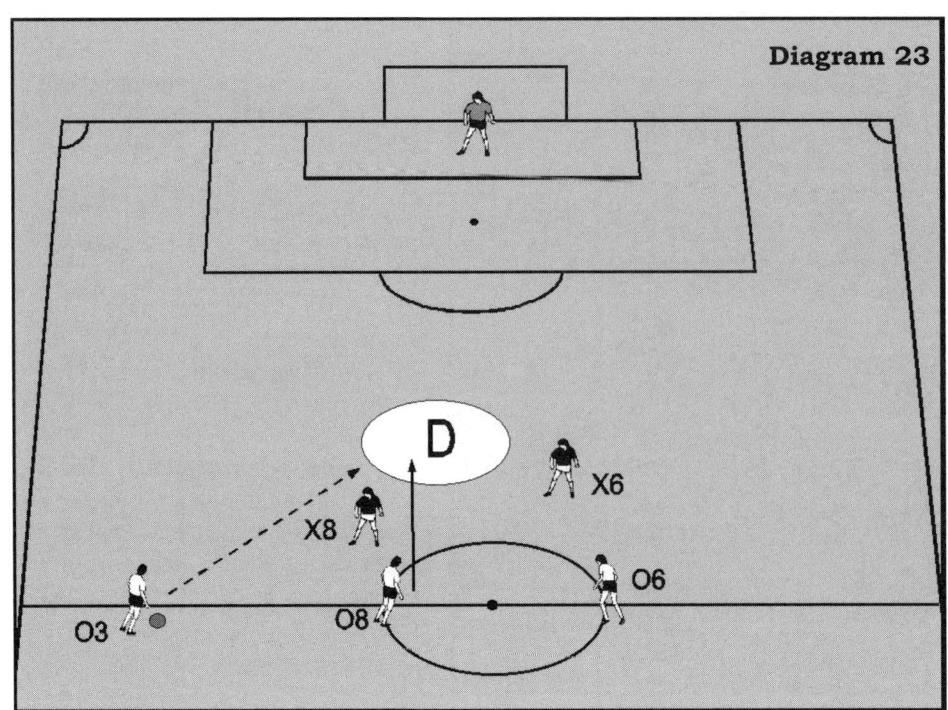

The midfielders play an important role to ensure that the back four are not over exposed to free-running midfielders.

X8 should take a position a little deeper and not get too tight on O8.

If X8 pushes up too tight on O8, it leaves the opportunity for space D to be exploited by a through-ball. X6 should also look to cover this in case 08 takes advantage or X8 is ball watching.

This is another situation that probably needs to be walked through by the coach.

The majority of teams these days, no matter what system they play, tend to show players inside when defending. However, once the back four reach the 18-yard line, more often than not the defending player will show the opponent outside. Such a tactic utilizes the end-line of the pitch where the attacking player is running out of space.

In this situation, the attacking team have still to get beyond the 18-yard line and the wide player (O7) in possession is being forced inside. Having done this, X4 needs to get as close as possible to O7. This forces O7 to put his head down and focus on the ball, which will limit his passing options.

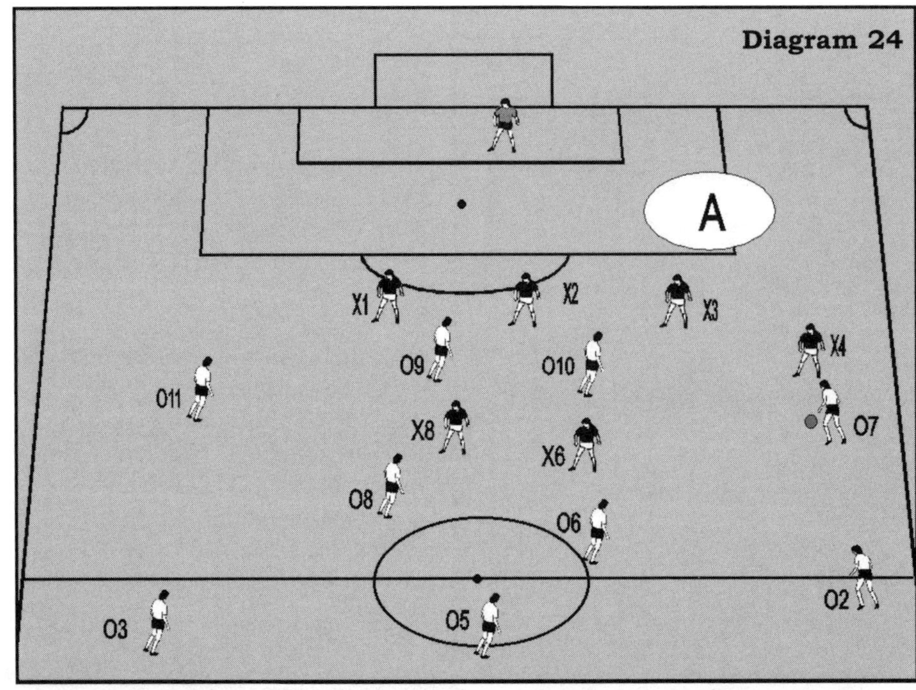

The 'line' is now set by X3 who needs to position himself close enough to X4 so that a pass into space A, in order to get past him, has to be so firm and straight that it will either run out of bounds or go through to the goalkeeper before O9 or O10 can get to it.

Because of X3's positioning, which makes it extremely difficult for O7 to pass behind the defense into space A, O7 is more likely to play a pass to the feet of O10 or O9, which invites X3 and X2 to come forward to make a challenge and not find themselves turned and facing their own goal.

Shows how space between X3 & X4 is crucial.

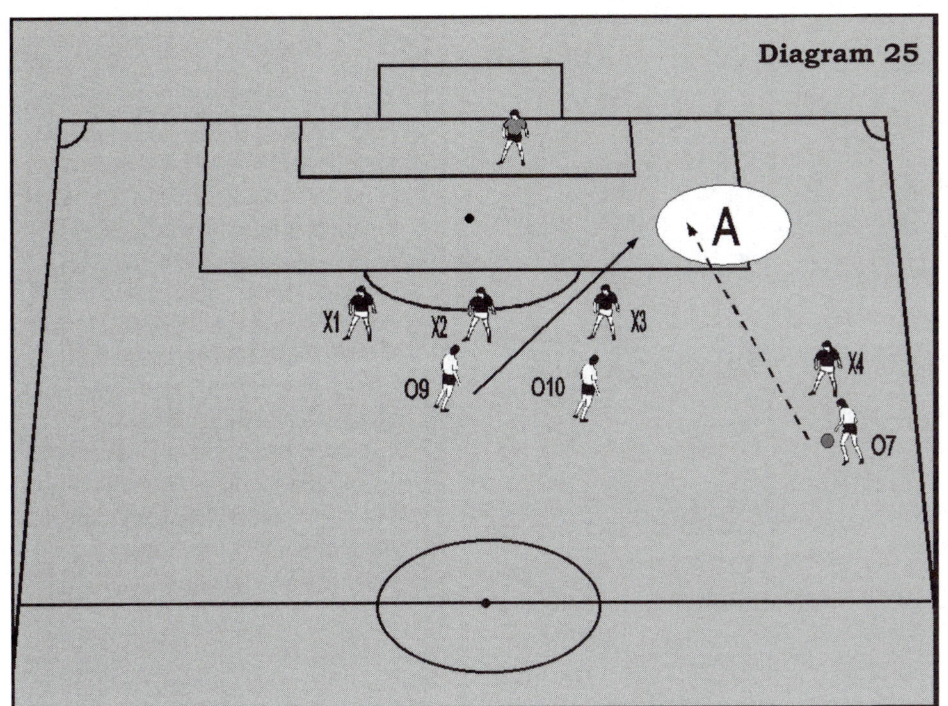

If X3 does not move far enough across, then a pass played into space A becomes a real possibility and a well timed run by an opponent (O9) puts them through on goal with only a goalkeeper to beat.

cp: covering defenders must drop back when defending high balls while ball is in air

Defending High Balls

The back four also have to deal with an aerial threat. There are going to be numerous occasions in any game where the opposition attack with long, high balls, sometimes just a long clearance by the goalkeeper. Indeed, some teams with tall strikers regularly use this ploy. The organization of the back four to counter this threat is very important.

The key to defending against an aerial attack is the covering position of the three defenders supporting the challenge so that one lost header does not lead to a strike on goal. Consider the following examples.

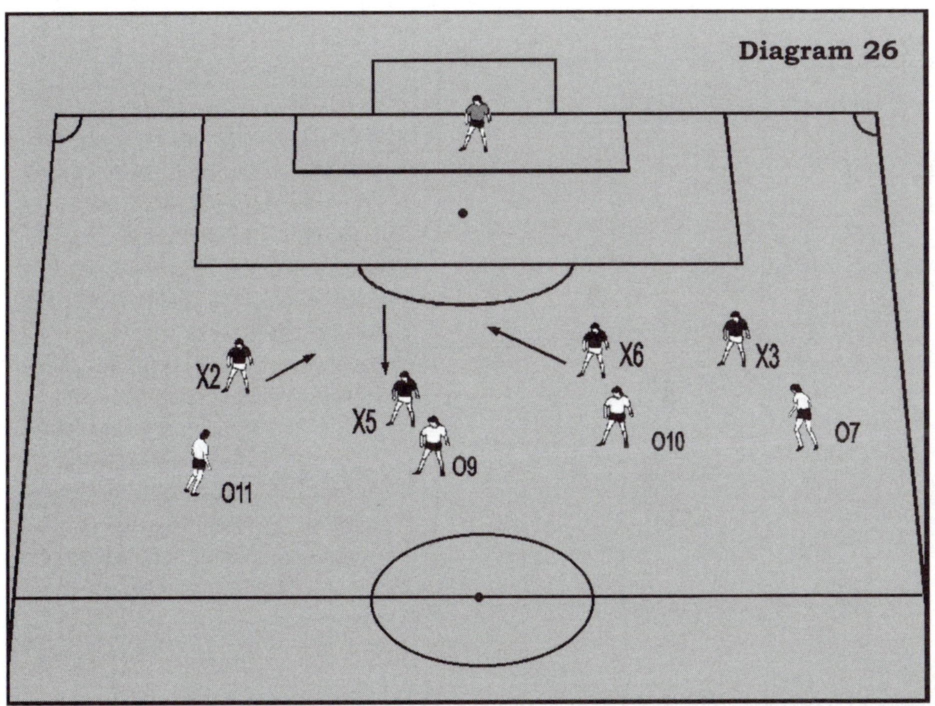

Correct

X 5 is challenging O9 in the air. X2 tucks in to cover the space behind X5 and so does X6. X3 also adjusts his position sensing that X6 has moved.

In this way, if O9 wins the header and flicks it on, one of the covering defenders should get to the ball first. If the ball drops to O11, O10 or O7, then the nearest defender can come forward to challenge and the team has not been turned to face their own goal.

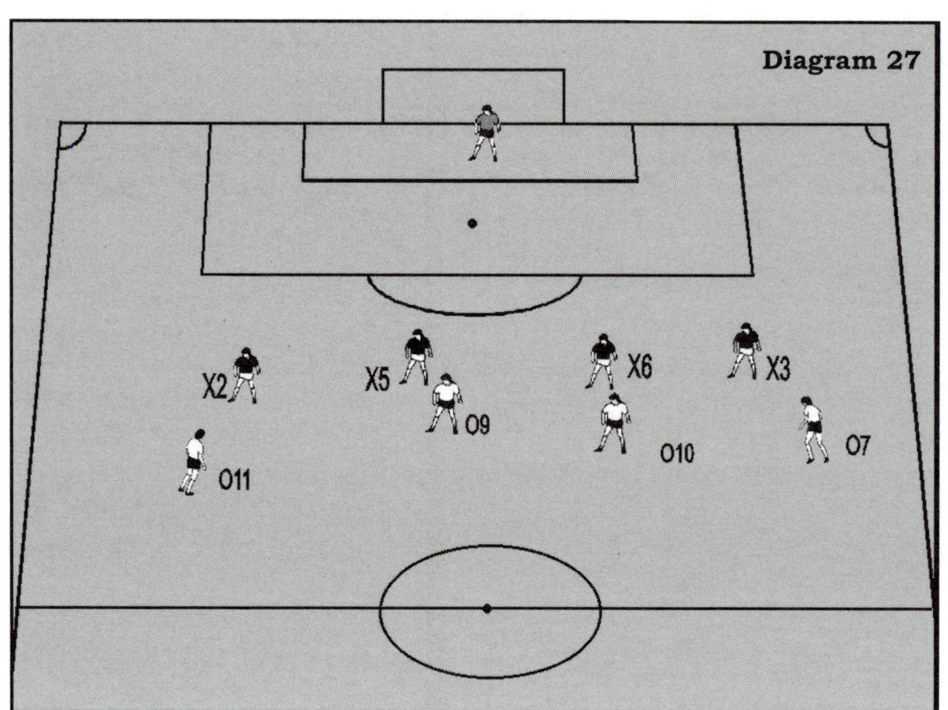

Incorrect

If the back four stays flat as shown, it can lead to a situation where if the forward wins the header, there is a good chance that one of the other forwards could get to the ball before a defender.

If X5 now challenges O9 for the ball in the air, and O9 is successful in touching it on, O11 and O10 may just have a chance of reaching the ball before a defender, creating a dangerous situation.

cp: whenever possible don't go out of zone to challenge high balls

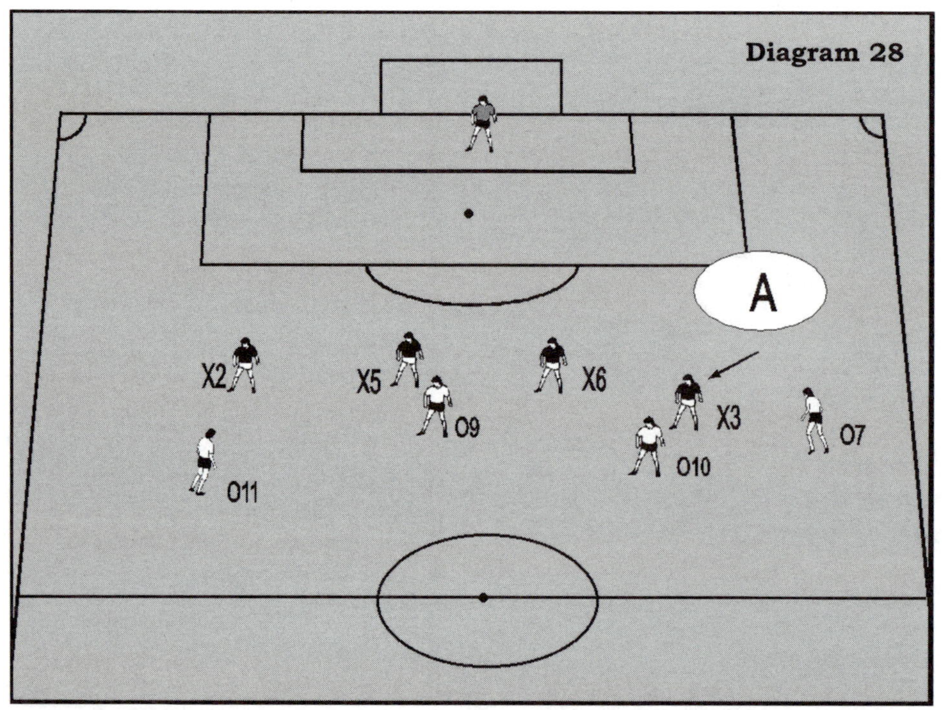

One other common problem with aerial challenges is for defenders to go for balls outside of their zone. In this example, X3 has decided to move inside to challenge O10 ahead of X6. This leaves a big space in which O7 now finds himself. If X3 wins the header then they may just get away with it. But if O10 is able to flick on towards O7, then this could cause problems since X6 is struggling to get across and deal with the threat.

English Premier League Comparisons

The principles of playing with a back four are identical or very similar at Manchester United, Arsenal, Liverpool or any team for that matter. Where differences do occur, is in the personnel involved and the demands of the coach.

Where the coach insists that the back four stay 'together' at all times and try to never break their shape, it's usually because of a cautious approach or the limitation of his players. In other words, he feels that they are there to defend first and foremost and should concentrate on that job. For the coaches with the more talented defenders, it is they who can influence the play of the back four.

Arsenal

Arsenal, for example, have England left back Ashley Cole. He has a great appetite to go forward and try to hurt the opposition with his attacking runs. So, although Arsenal will follow the principles of defending we have discussed, they will not want to stifle Cole's attacking threat.

Consequently, the team, and especially the other three members of the back four (Campbell, Keown and Lauren), adjust to Cole's raids down the left side

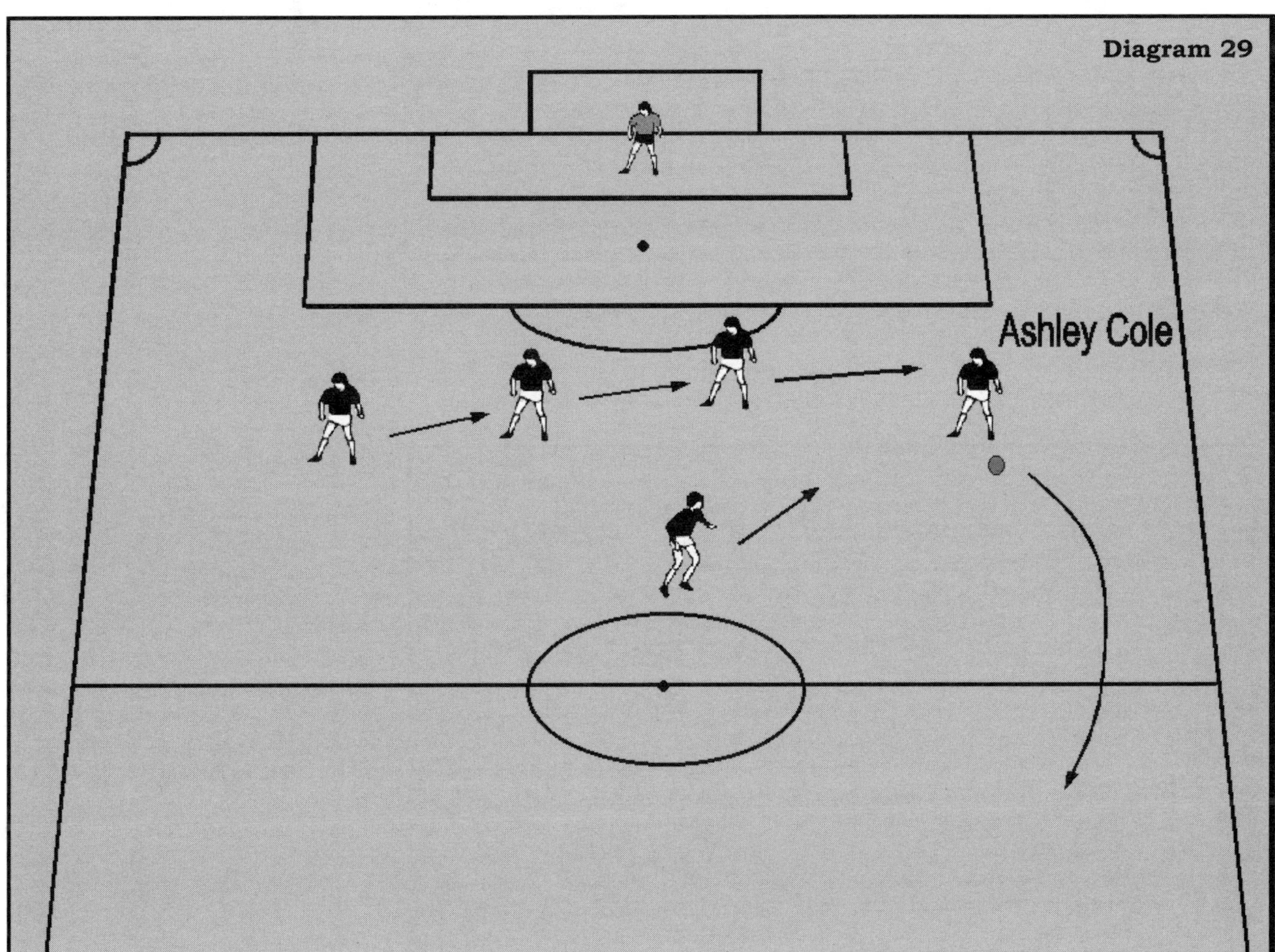

When Cole makes a forward run, the other three defenders slide across as shown.

If the right fullback has also gone forward, then a midfielder (Patrick Vierra) will drop back.

Manchester United

Manchester United have fullbacks more like Cole, and they have the freedom to go forward and cause problems for the opposition. Silvestre on the left and Gary Neville on the right go forward at every opportunity. In this, they are often assisted by Giggs and Beckham who deliberately make movements infield in order to create space for their fullbacks to go forward.

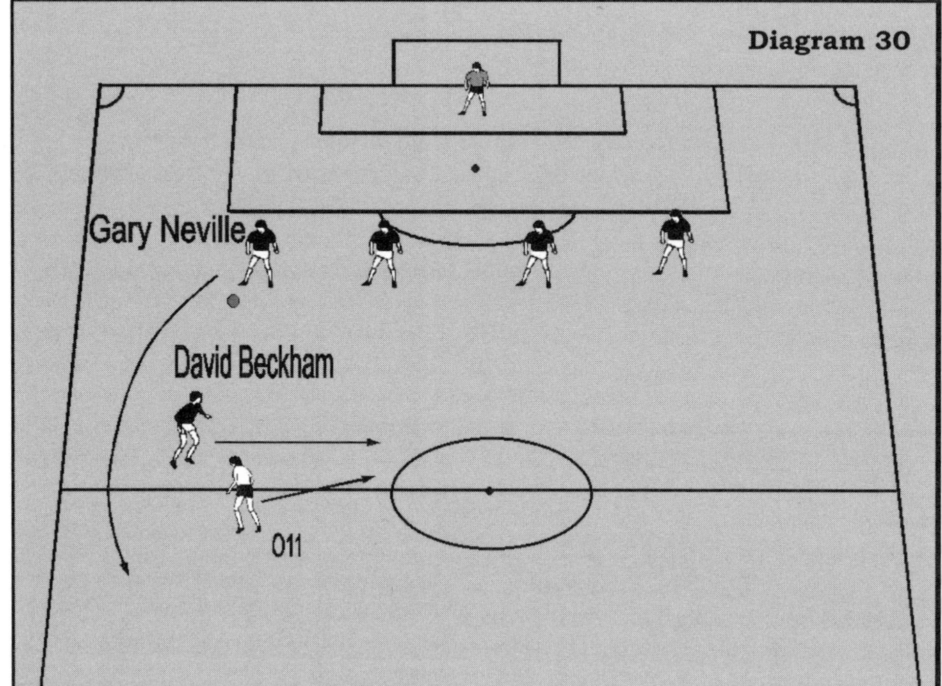

Beckham on the right (Giggs on the left) often run inside to give their markers a problem.

If O11 stays with Beckham, he leaves space for Neville to attack the flank.

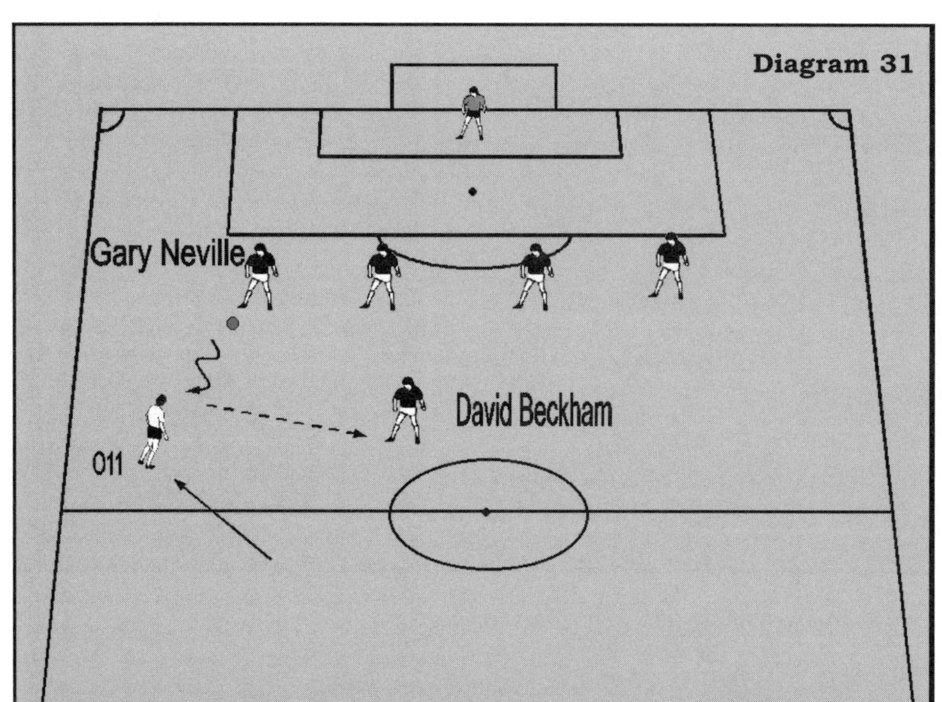

If O11 stays wide to cover the run by Neville, he then leaves Beckham free inside.

The ambition of every coach is to construct a team where every player is comfortable in possession of the ball. Thus, for the center backs, when the defending is done, and they are required to possess the ball and initiate attacking play, the coach is looking for them to sometimes come out and attack with the ball.

Manchester United probably have the best options in this respect. Rio Ferdinand, the world's most expensive defender, is extremely comfortable in running the ball out, passing the ball accurately into midfield or stepping forward to join in an attack at the right time.

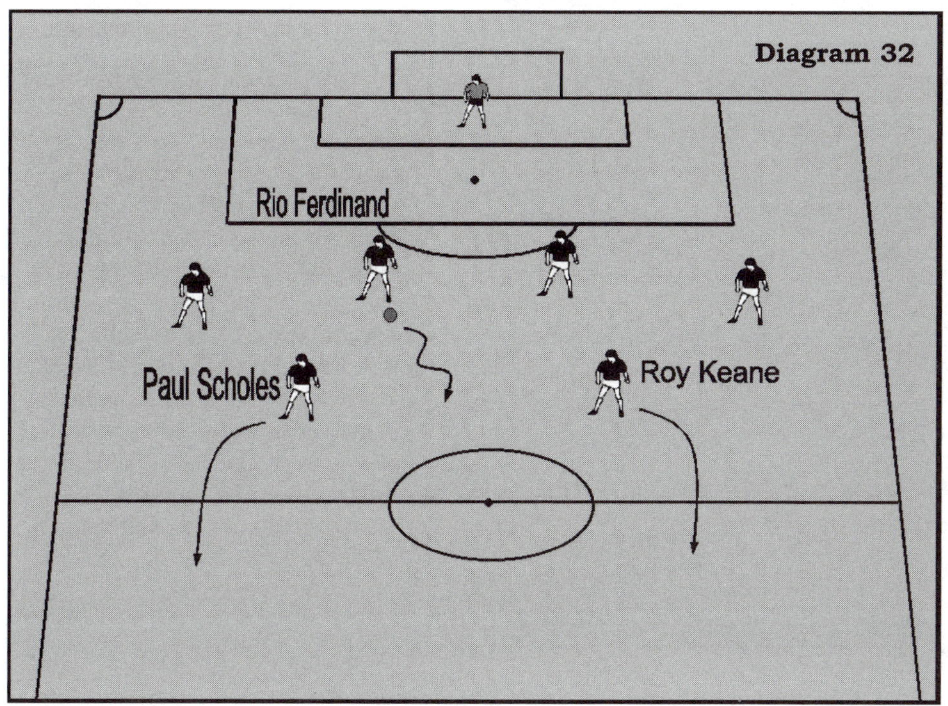

Ferdinand, when in possession in deep areas, will often bring the ball forward into the space between the opposing strikers. This allows the midfield players (Keane, Scholes, Veron) to push further up the field causing more problems for the opposing defenders.

At Arsenal, Campbell and Keown have become better at this as have Hyppia and Henchoz at Liverpool. However, at Manchester United, not only do they have Ferdinand, but alongside him, Blanc, who is coolness personified with the ball at his feet.

While this aspect of a center backs game continues to become more important, the priority for all defenders are their defensive duties. These must be addressed first.

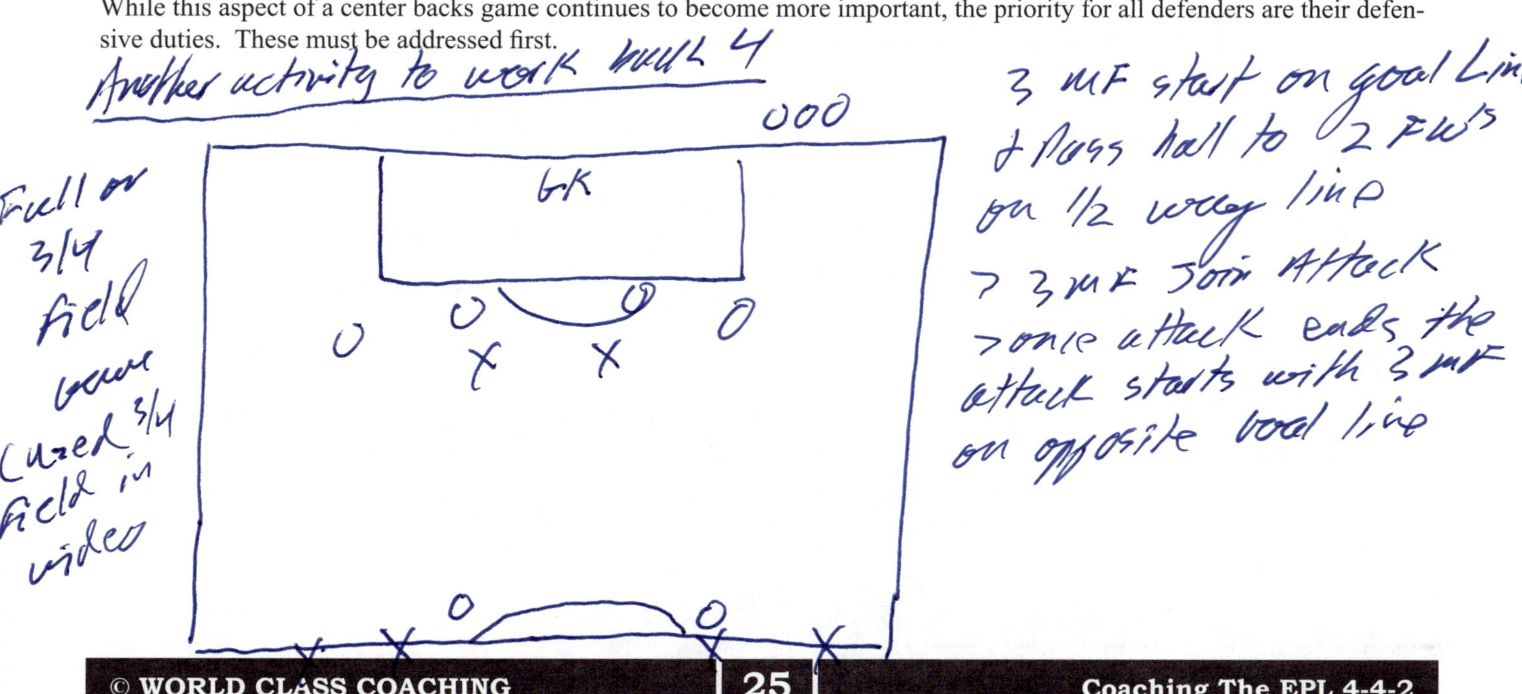

Press or Deep?

Within the defensive strategy of the coach is the 'positioning' of the back four. There are basically two choices: Play with the back four pushed up or play with the back four deep. I think it would be fair to say that the world's best teams, with the most talented and intelligent players, are good enough to use the appropriate tactics on a game by game basis.

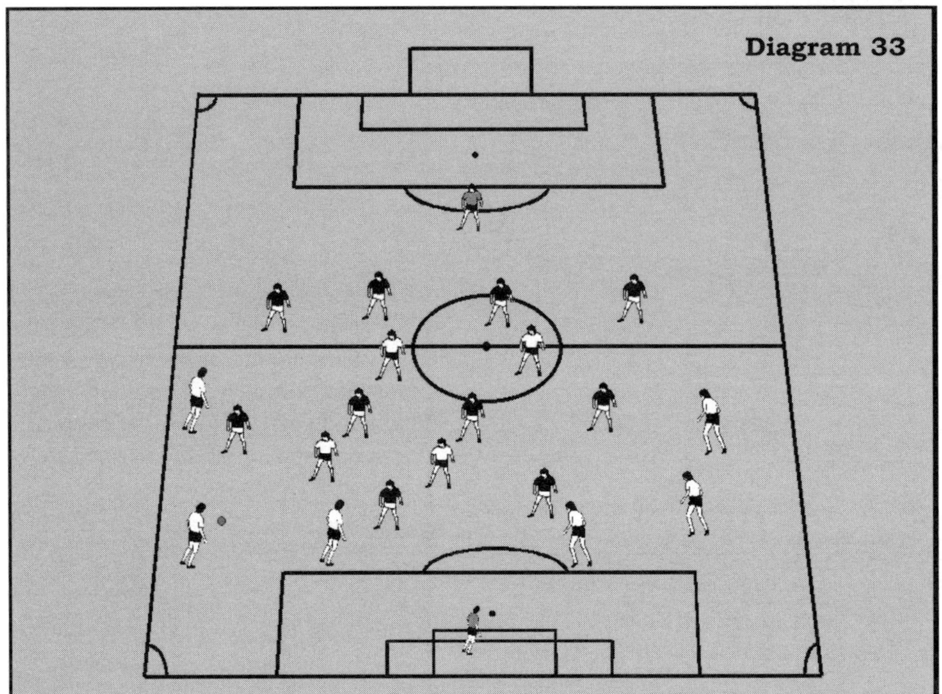

High Back Four

To play the back four 'high' - close to the halfway line - is a tactic known as 'pressing'. The result of this is to push the midfielders and strikers further up the pitch and congest the play as close to the oppositions goal as possible.

In order to play this way, the back four needs to have quick players since playing high leaves space behind and the defenders need to be first to any ball over the top. Such a tactic also requires the goalkeeper to be alert and act as a sweeper.

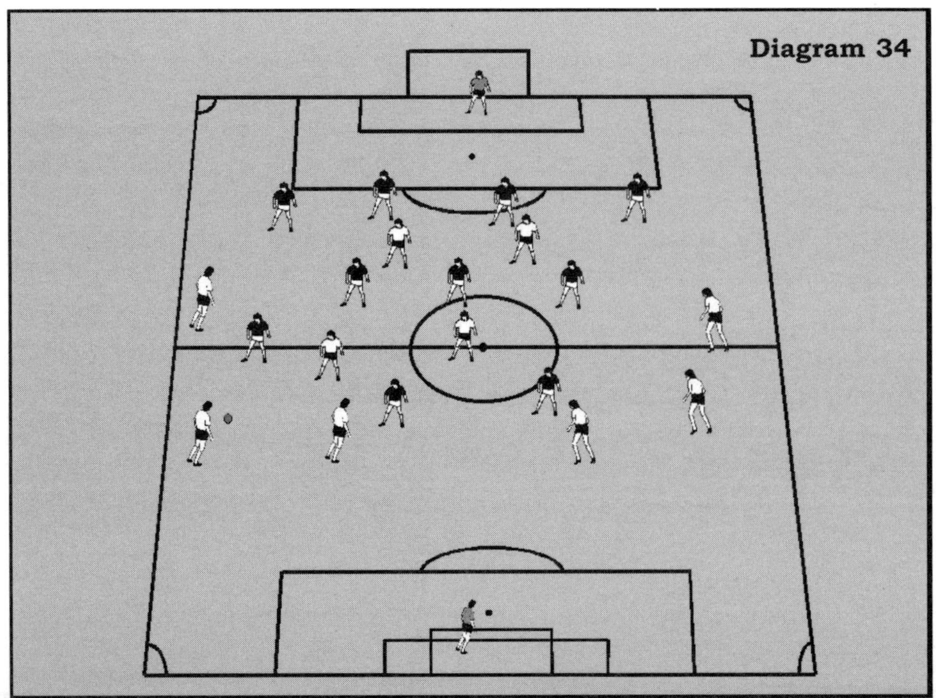

Deep Back Four

The back four can also defend deep, leaving limited space between the back line and the GK. It might also be useful where the pace of the back four players is questionable or the strength of the opposition is their quick forwards who thrive on space to run into.

This is a tactic for teams who are adept at counter-attacking by drawing the opposition forward and hitting them on the break.

Chapter Two

Defending With The Midfield Four

"Games are won and lost in midfield" so the expression goes, and it is easy to see why. A team that dominates in this area can thwart the opposing attacks before they even test their own back four and provide the launch pad for their own offensive play. Hence the role of the midfield four and their defensive duties is critical to the success of the team.

The basics of defending for midfield players can be practiced in the early 2 v 2 practices explained in Chapter One. There is also some merit in spending time with the midfield quartet using practices from the previous chapter. In this way, the midfield players can understand their relative positions when attacked through the middle or down the flanks.

Apart from these two suggestions, most of the defensive play with the midfield four needs to include the back four and goalkeeper. Therefore, some of the initial work can be started using the practices from diagrams 16 and 20 from the previous chapter.

In both these functions two central midfield players are involved. The central midfielders must understand from the outset the need to play together.

Once the coach is confident that the back four defenders are sure of their roles, he can start to work with the two central midfield players using the following set-up.

In this situation, O3 has the ball. This requires X8 and X6 to move across to that side of the pitch. They must move as 'one unit' or they will be ineffective.

start with 8v6 then 10v8 to add outside MF

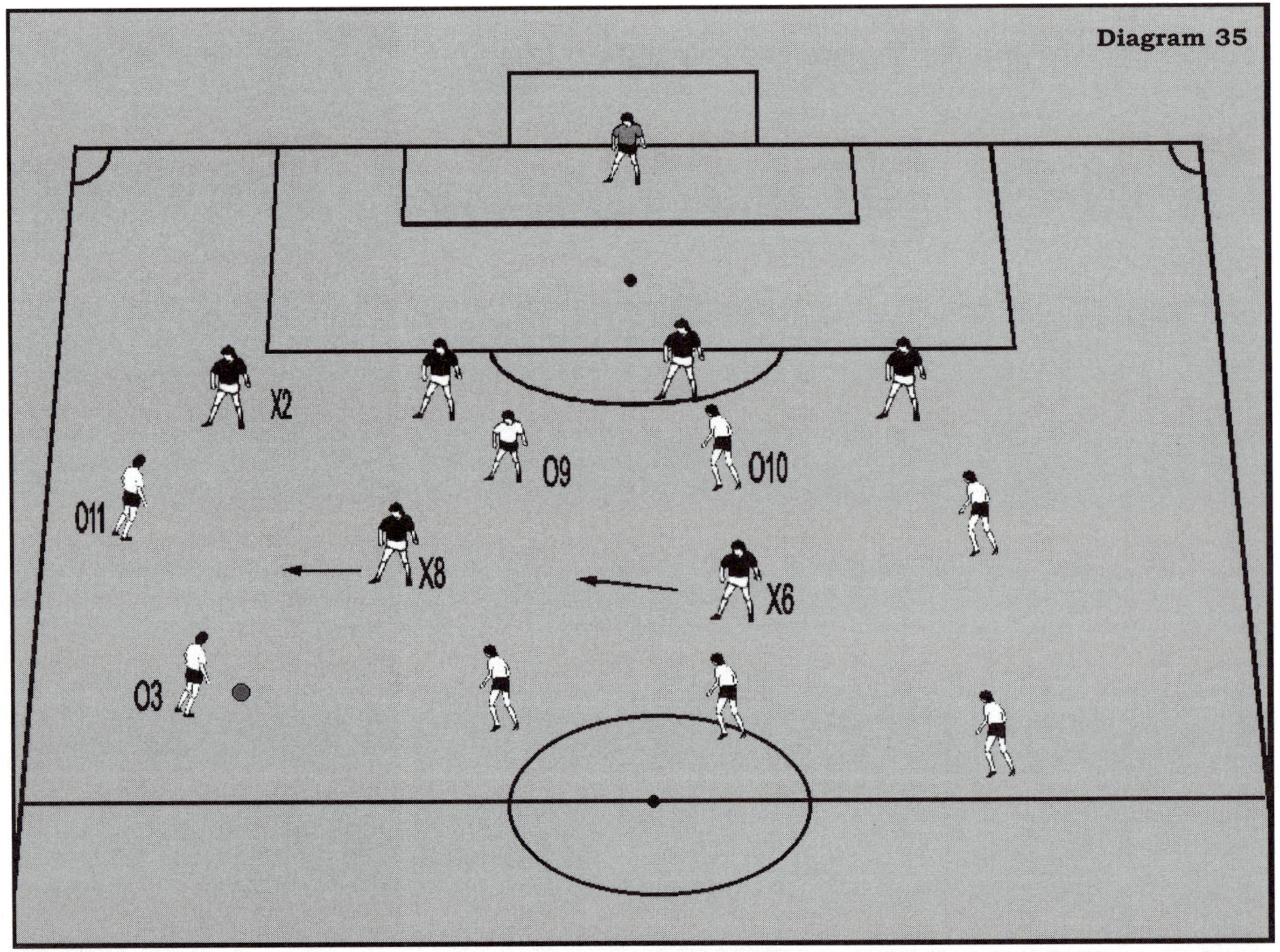

Diagram 35

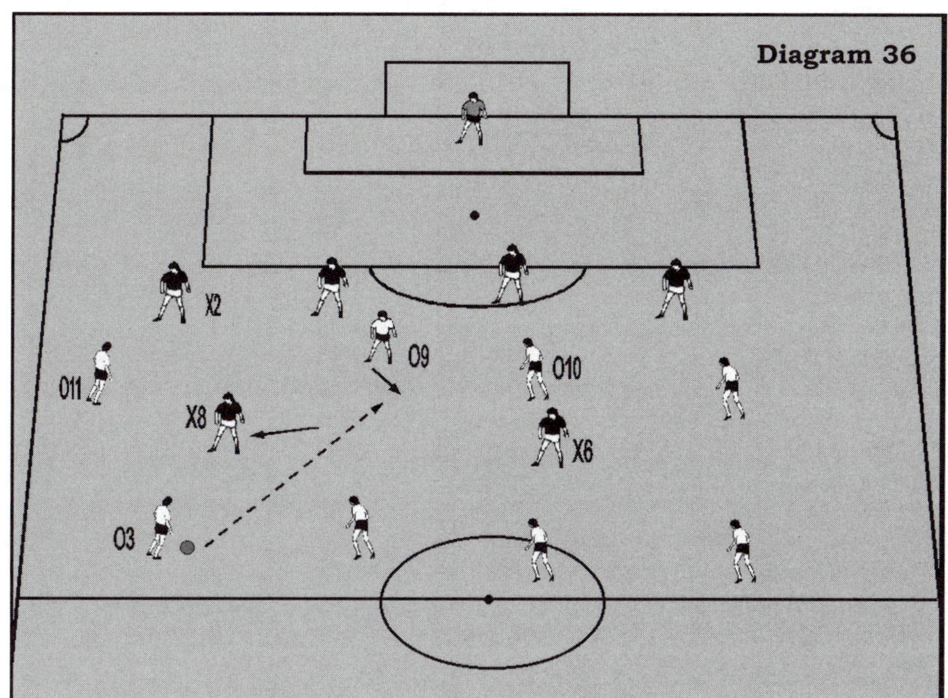

If X8 moves alone and X6 stays, that leaves a gap that can be exploited with a pass into the forwards.

CP: must work together, not too close or too far apart

Aside: 8v6: Attackers include 2FW, 2OM even or behind Defensive MF; 2 CM and 2OD's in front of Defensive CM. FW's are on line 1/2 way between PK box and MF.

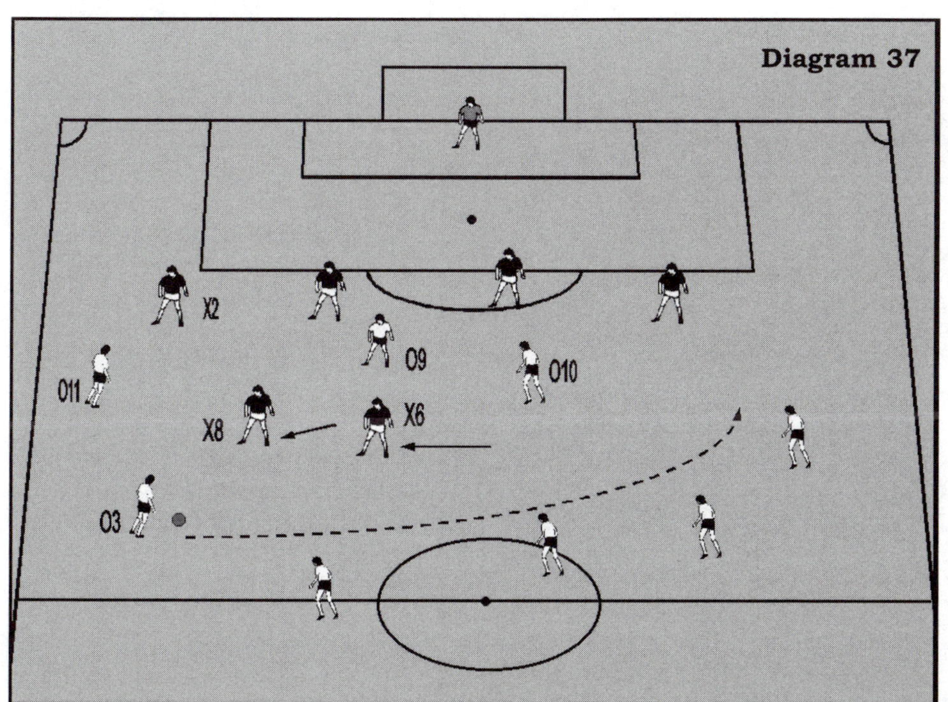

If X6 follows X8 too closely, then a pass across the field could leave them exposed on the opposite flank.

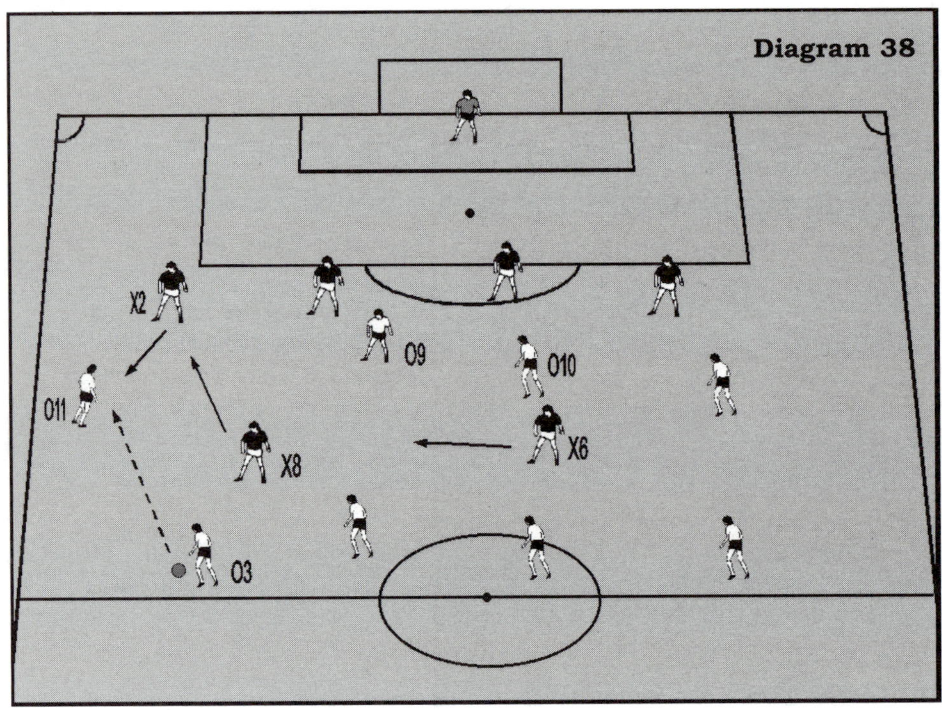

Ideally, X8 positions himself to block a pass to O9 but accepting that O11 could receive the ball and that he could then support X2 (see 2 v 2 practice).

NB: X8 must deny pass to FW (O9) + concede pass to O11

As mentioned earlier, it is critical that X8 and X6 move together as a unit. X6 moving across will also stop the ball being played either O9 or O10. In this way, the two central midfield players have delayed the attack and 'bought' time for other players to recover their defending positions.

Of course the coach would hope that his team discipline would not allow this situation to occur too often, but if it did, then the way he has schooled his players limits the chances of exploitation.

The next step is to add the two wide midfield players so that the midfield quartet is complete. Continuing with a 10 v 8 practice as shown, attention needs to be given to the midfield four as a unit.

NB: Added Attacking CM per video

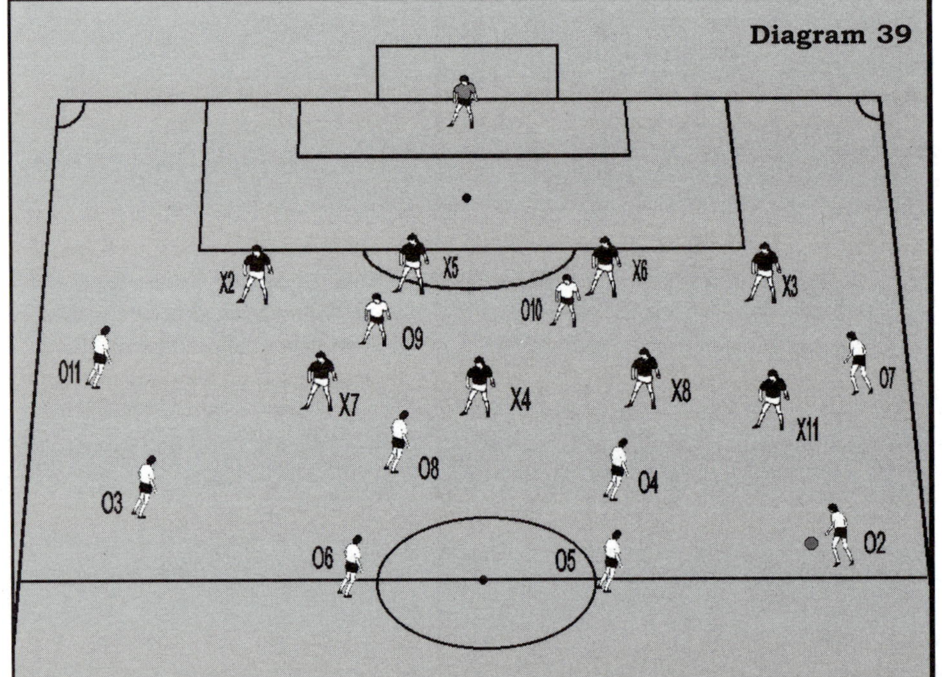

In this practice, the coach again must spend time organizing his players when the ball is in certain parts of the field. For example, if O2 has the ball, first check that the back four are in the correct positions and then move on to the midfield.

The coach must also check that the space between the defenders and midfielders isn't too close or too far apart.

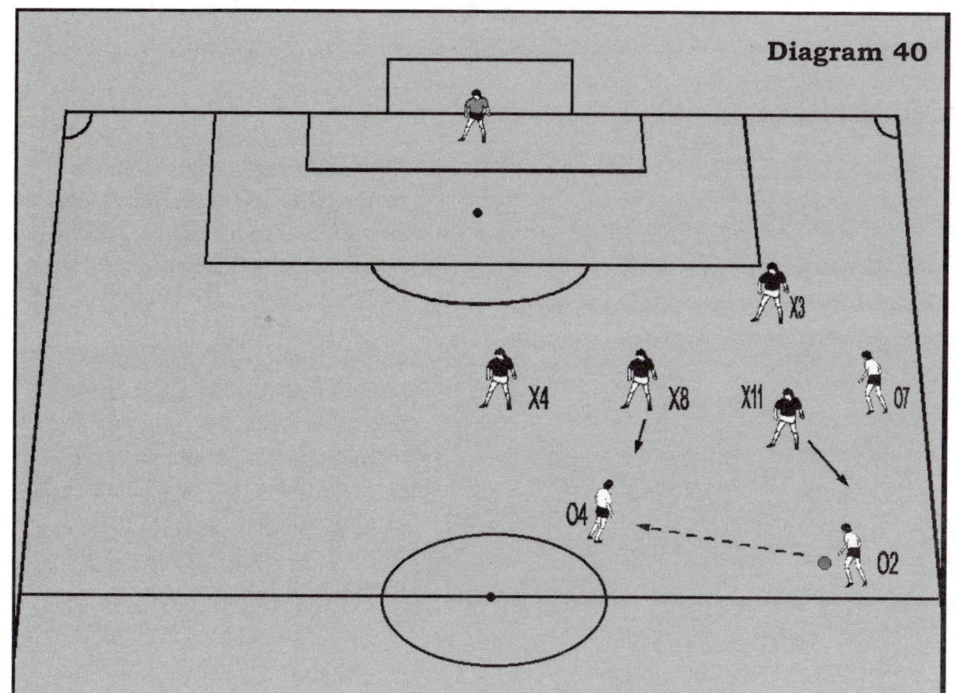

X11 should encourage O2 to inside by cutting of the pass to O7. If he does not, then a pass to 07 puts the ball behind the midfield four and they all have to turn, which means they lose sight of their opponent.

By making O2 play inside, the ball stays in front of the midfield.

LP: Whenever possible force ball inside.

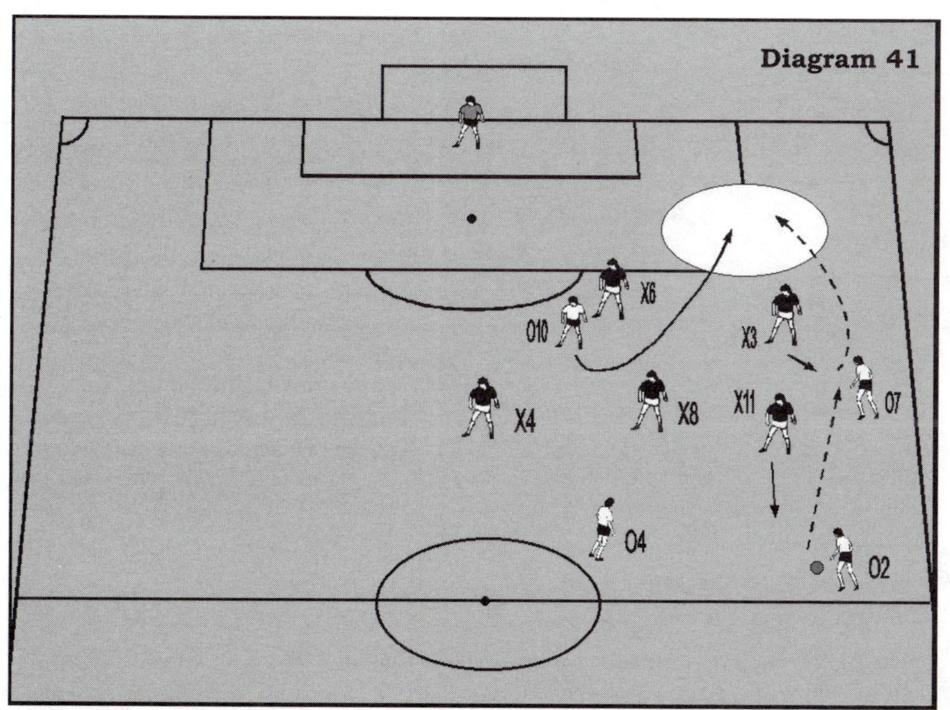

Forcing O2 to play inside also allows X3 to stay in the 'hole'. If X11 allows O2 to pass wide to O7, X3 then has to leave his position and defend O7. This leaves a hole, which the strikers O9 or O10 might try to exploit.

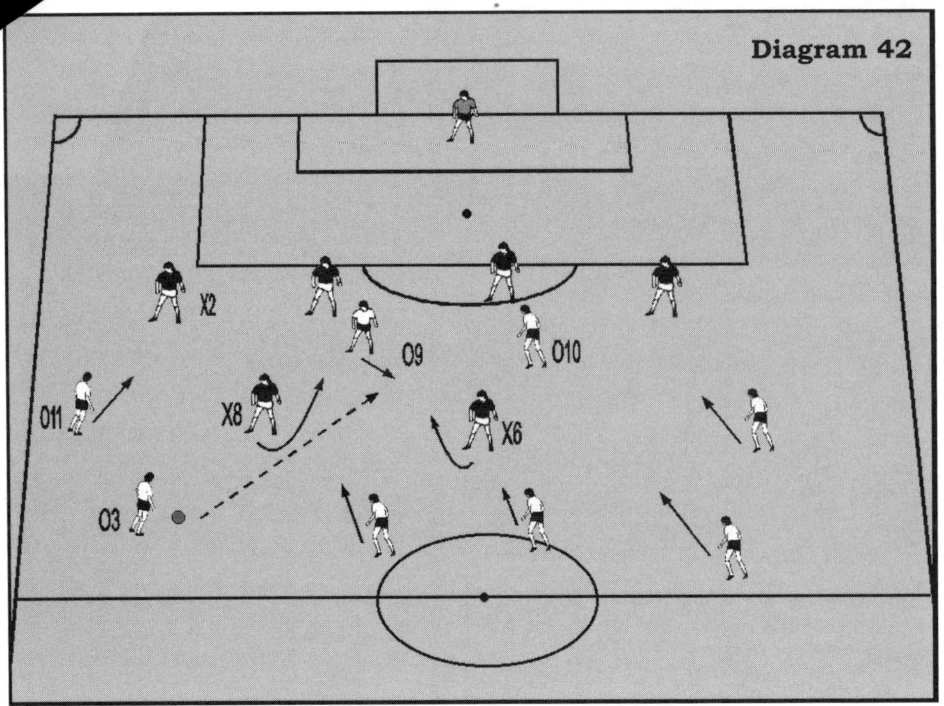

Diagram 42

As we have mentioned earlier, X8 needs to stop a pass into the strikers (O9 and O10), but if he is unable to, then he and X6 need to 'back tackle' as early as possible. Failure to do so, and leaving a striker comfortable in possession, will encourage the opposition midfielders to make forward runs beyond the ball. Such movement by the opposing midfielders will be thwarted if they sense that back tackling midfield players may win the ball before it has a chance to be passed to them.

By back tackling, the CM's discourage attacking MF's from making forward runs because they won't think the FW can get them the ball.

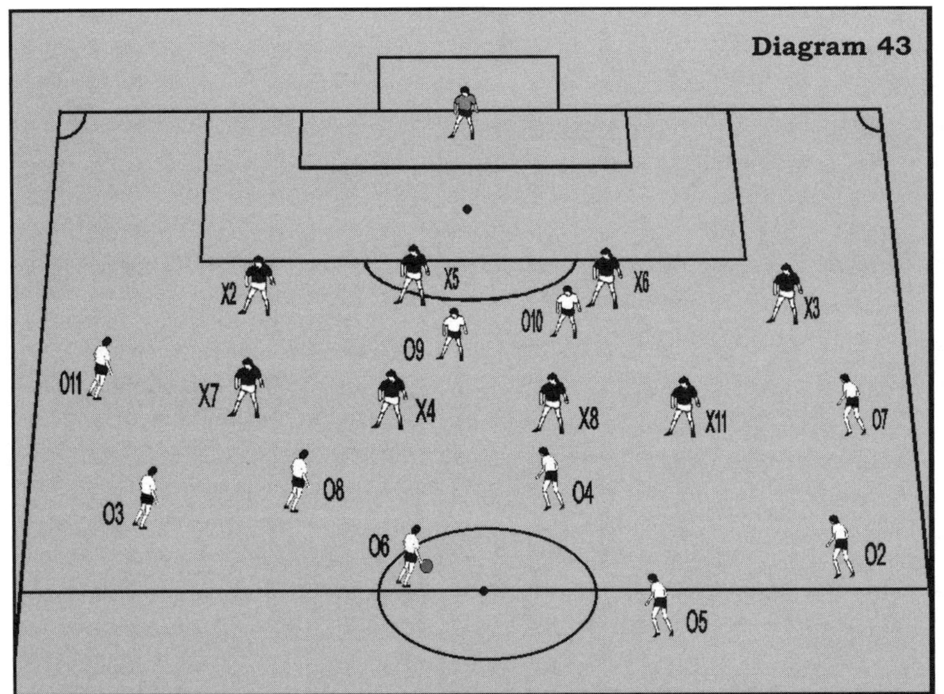

Diagram 43

In this situation, the ball is in the middle of the field with a center defender (O6). When the ball is central, it is important that the four midfielders start to "narrow" and squeeze closer together as shown.

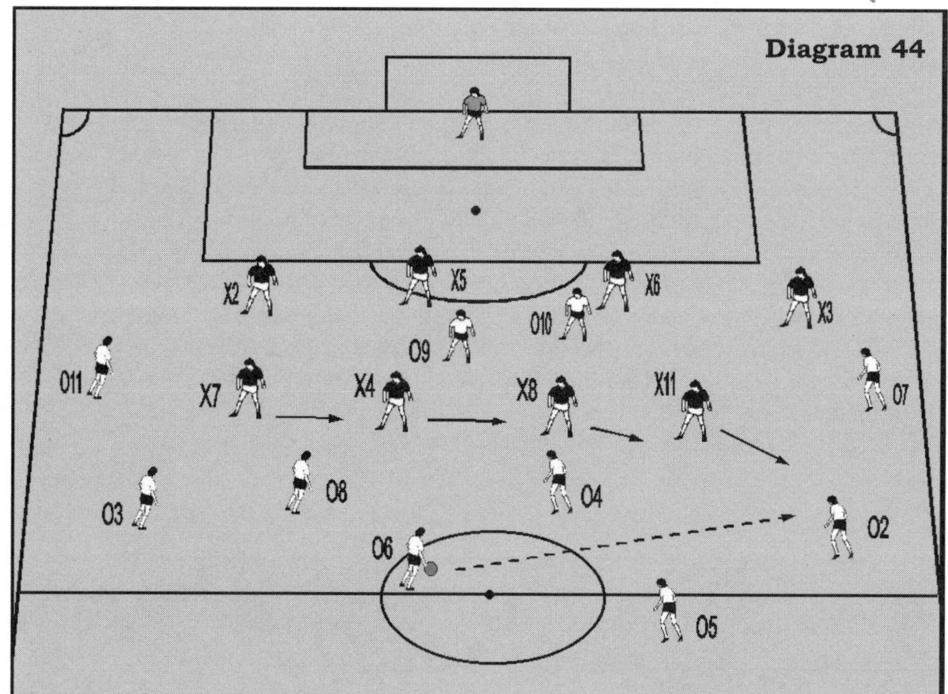

If the ball is passed out wide, the midfielders should shift sideways to react to the change in point of attack.

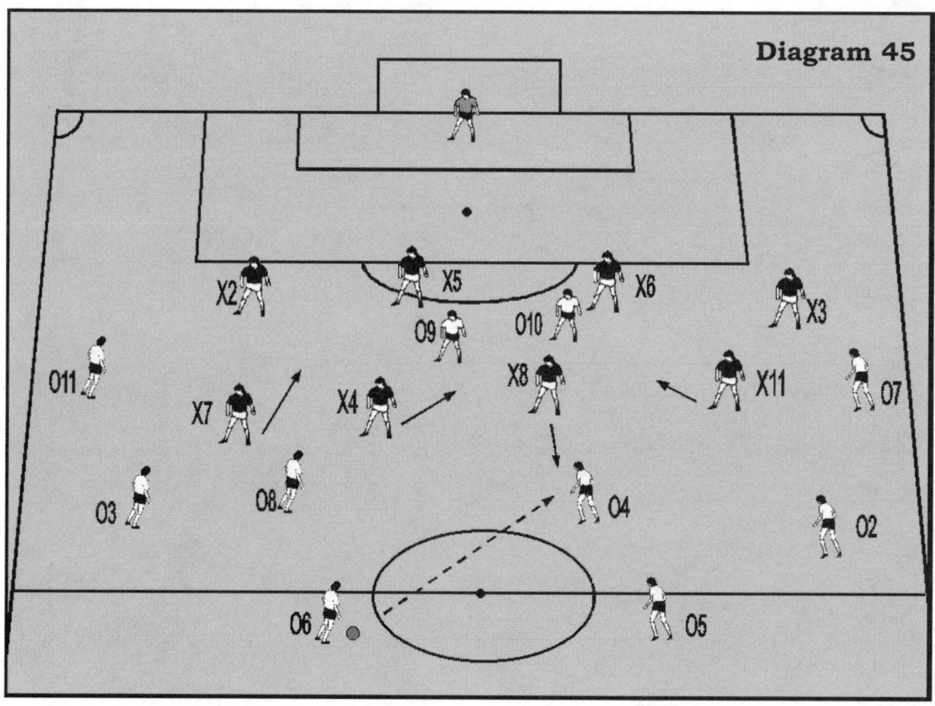

If the ball is passed forward to a midfielder, the closest player should step up and pressure the ball (X8). The other three midfielders should take up the appropriate support positions as shown and described for the back four defenders in diagram 11.

This 10 v 8 practice should be practiced regularly, the more it is practiced the more habit forming it becomes. The coach, once the practice goes 'live', needs to instigate wave after wave of attacks against his back four and his midfield four remembering that each time they win possession they need a target to play to and also to move forward together as ONE unit.

Of course it is unrealistic to think that the shape of the team will always be this perfect. There will always be occasions when players are out of position. To allow for this, the midfield players especially must be able to fill in directly for those defenders behind them when needed. For instance, when the right back has gone forward and play breaks down, the right side midfield player must be capable of assuming his position. Likewise, a center back drawn forward and caught out of position, needs to be able to rely on a central midfield colleague to take his place.

To help understand the different responsibilities of the midfielders and how and who they should cover for, the coach can employ the following practice for his players.

In this practice, the coach designates one of the midfield players as the "out of position midfielder, and has him stand next to him. In this example, X11 is the midfield player out of position. The coach then starts the practice off as before but 'holds' X11 until the ball is in play for a second or two. By starting the practice down the right side of the pitch (X11's defending side), the coach can now work with the remaining midfield players on how to cover for their out of position colleague.

By constant repetition, using all four midfield players in turn, and with plenty of variations, the midfield four should recognize that there are four slots to be filled. And at any time when they are making recovery runs after a change of possession, they need to position themselves in the nearest one. After that, they need to be able to cope with the demands of the position, if only for a brief time, until the team recovers its shape.

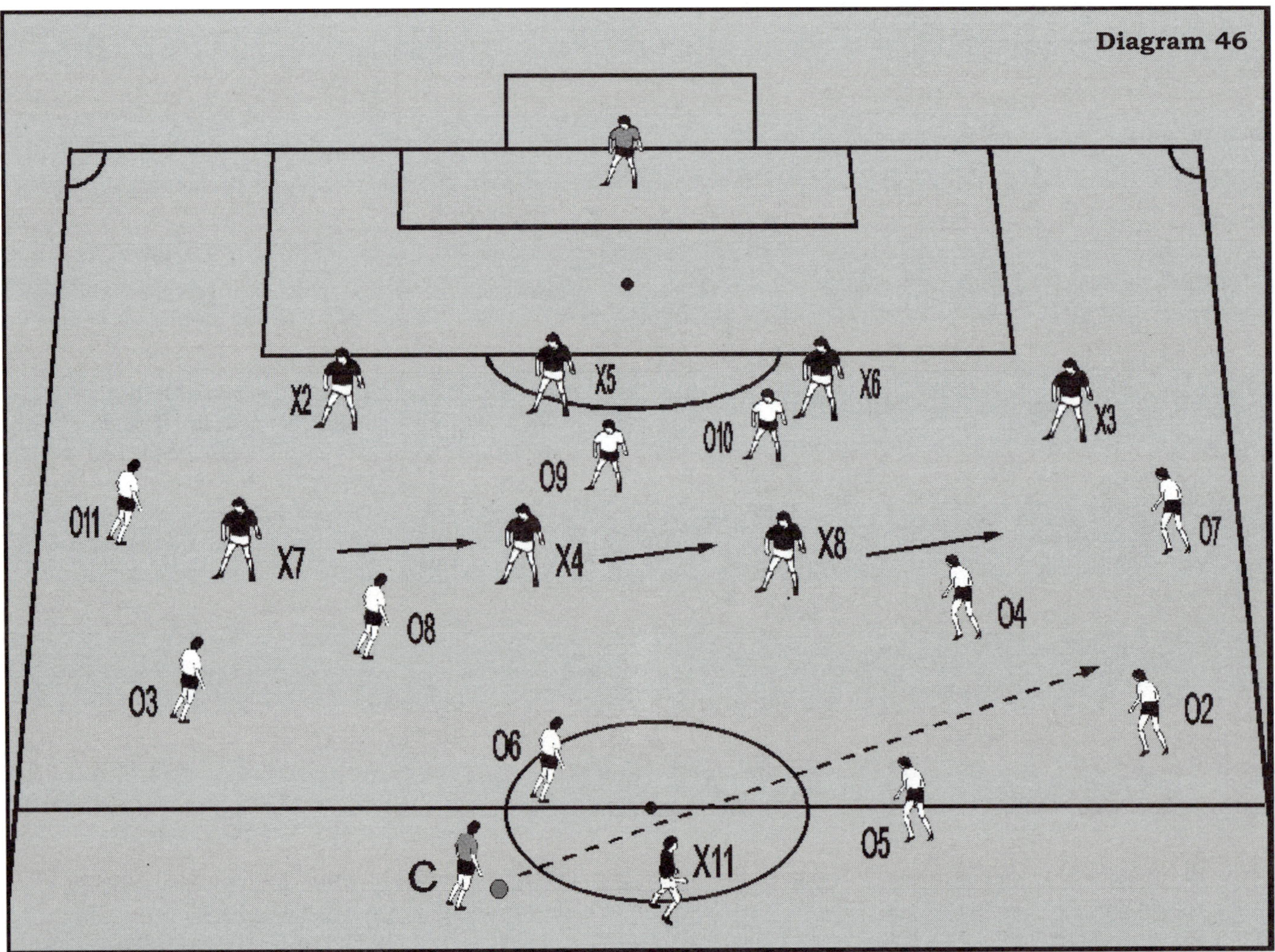

NB: Forwards are on top of circle on 18 whereas they where on line 1/2 way between midfield and 18 for 8 v 6

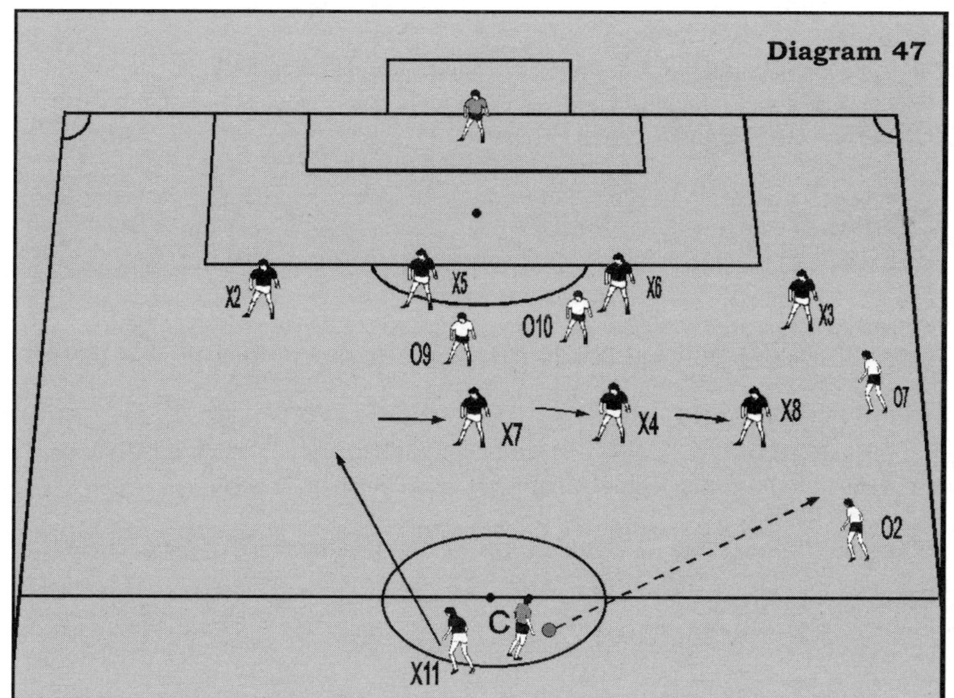

Diagram 47

Once the coach has passed the ball in, X8, followed by X4, need to slide across . X7 must then assess his position, depending on when the coach decides to release X11. On release, X11 must look to recover the nearest vacant gap in the midfield four. If X7 has moved it may be that X11 becomes a wide right player.

An Great way to train as group is 11 v 3 with 3 players passing back + forth just past midfield. The Back four are position slightly deeper than 1/2 way between midfield and top of PK box. Then add FW + CM to attack. Conditions are you pressure but don't tackle. Once attack is stalled they bring it back out.

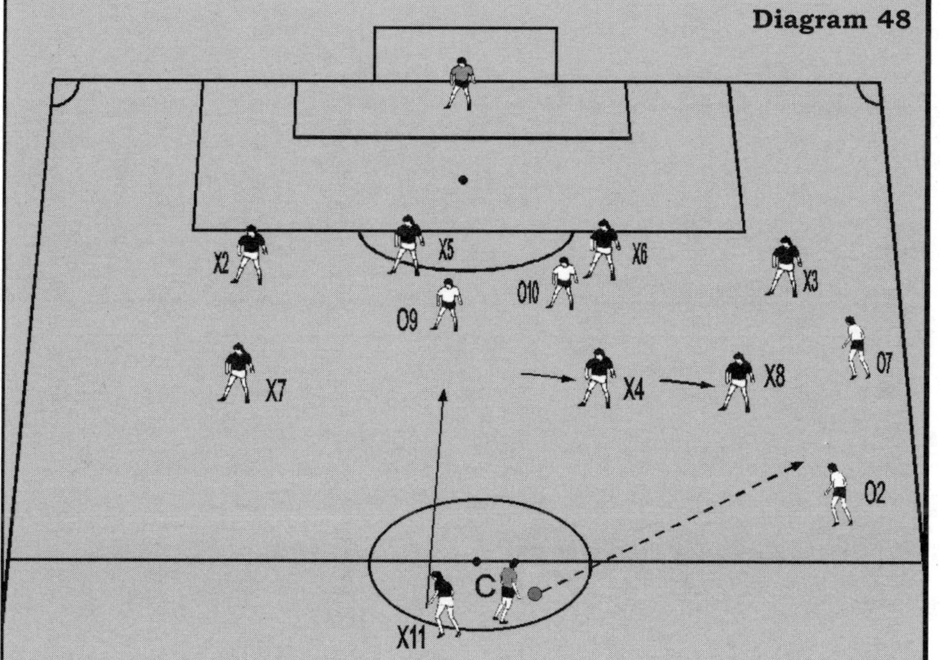

Diagram 48

If X7 has maintained his position and not moved over, the X11 should look to fill in the gap between X7 and X4.

The coach can also test the back four by holding one of the defenders out of position to see how the team copes with that disruption. By repeatedly asking different questions the coach can help the players adjust and make the correct decisions.

English Premier League Comparisons

In much the same way as with the back four, the giants of the English Premier League insist that their midfield players follow the principles laid down of how to defend as a unit. They may be flexible when in possession, but it is critical that the midfielder's know their responsibility immediately their team loses possession.

However, the individual strengths of certain players are also to be seen. For example, at Liverpool, Hamann the German international, who performed well in the 2002 World Cup, is excellent at screening and protecting his back four. He achieves this in two ways - see diagrams.

Hamann is mainly considered the 'anchor' man and this allows the likes of Steven Gerrard and Danny Murphy, both England internationals, a greater degree of freedom since they know that the Hamann will always be ready to fill in for them.

Liverpool differ slightly than Manchester United or Arsenal in that they do not have a 'dribbler' in the mould of Giggs or Pires on the wings and consequently their midfield four is often naturally narrower than United or Arsenal.

Therefore, where one or two wingers are included in your team, midfielders recovery runs and the shape of the midfield four needs to be worked at especially hard.

In this example, Hamann will do what he does best, which is read the intended pass to the forward. Quite often he is successful and able to intercept the pass.

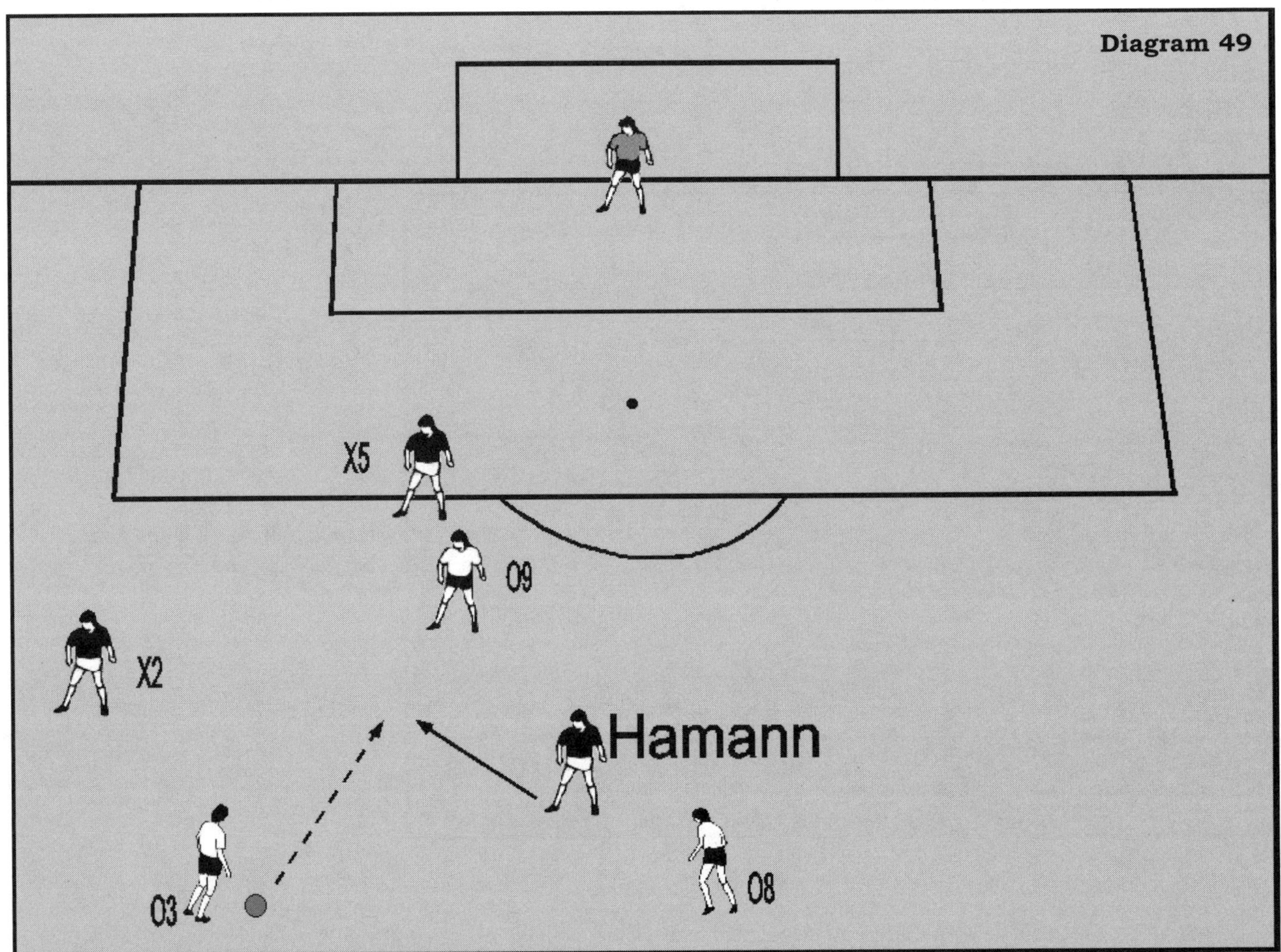

In this example, Hamann isn't able to intercept the pass. When this happens, he is very quick to pressure the forward from the "wrong" side. Therefore, the forward has to try and shield the ball from the defender (X5) but knows that if he does that it "shows" the ball toward the back tackling Hamann.

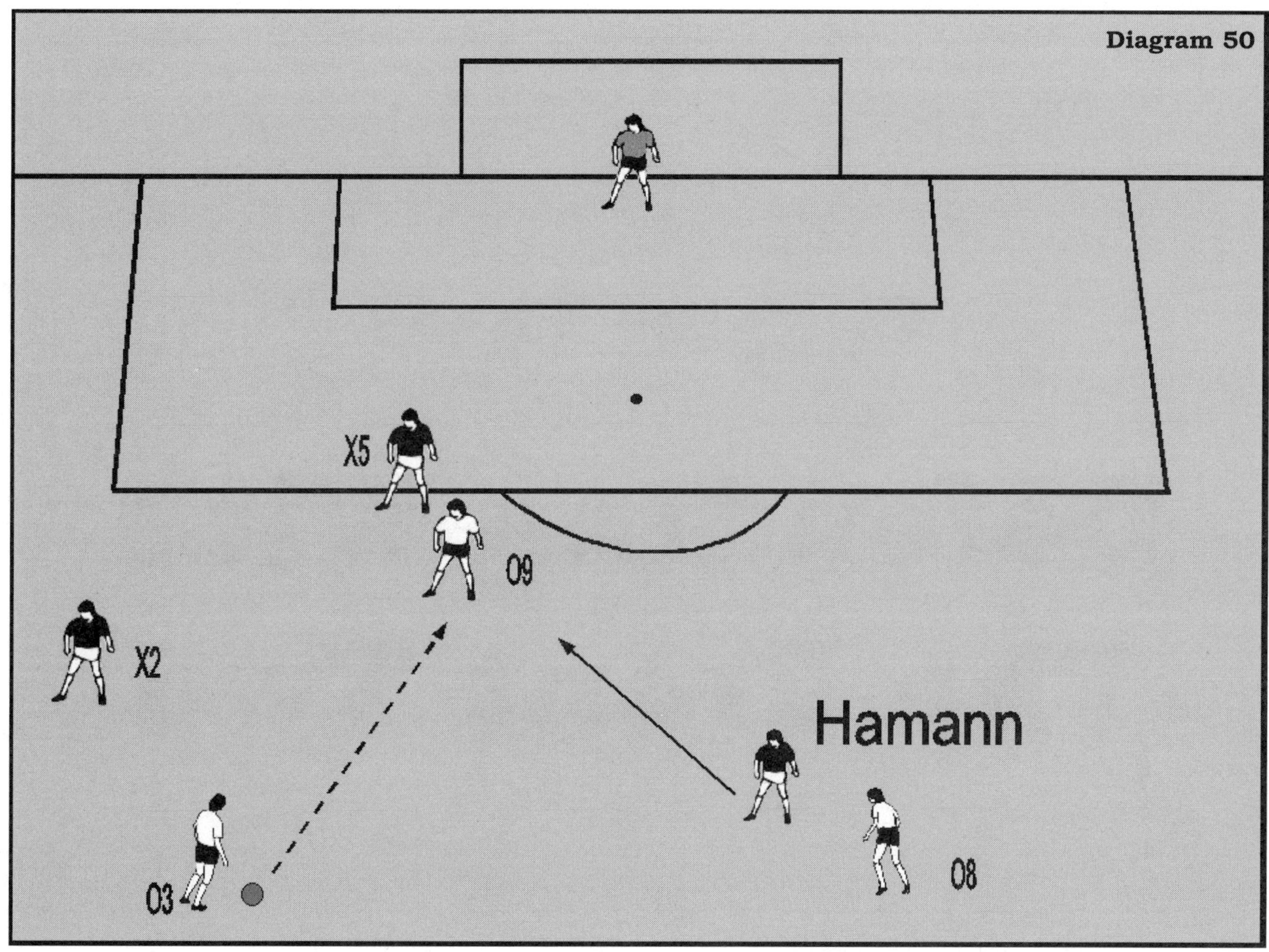

At Manchester United, although Keane is extremely good at doing this job, it is too limiting for him. He needs to be in the game at all times and is likely to turn up anywhere on the pitch when United have the ball. Patrick Vierra at Arsenal comes into the same category and both United and Arsenal have good balance to their midfield four.

For United, Beckham and Giggs work extremely hard down the flanks and assist their respective fullbacks in their defensive duties. Although the strength of both players is in their attacking qualities, they recognize the importance of filling holes when the team is defending, as well as supporting the challenges of other team members.

Arsenal have the same work ethic from their flank players whose strengths again are their creative ability. Pires from France, Ljungberg the Swede, who can play on either flank and Parlour from England, another wide player, all do exceptional jobs for the team.

Chapter Three

Defending With The Front Two

Soccer has evolved into a game where at the top level, the 10 outfield players need to attack together and defend together. So, although the strikers are not selected for their defensive prowess, they do have an important role to play when their team is not in possession. The days of strikers being virtual spectators when their team doesn't have the ball are long gone.

However, there are a number of variables to consider when examining the defensive role of the two strikers. First, the coach has to decide how his TEAM will defend. When discussing the back four, we mentioned defending high and pressing as a team strategy or defending deep and denying the opposition space behind the back four. We will examine both options.

Second, the strikers are the only unit of the team likely to be outnumbered when it comes to defending. The two forwards could be playing against four or three defenders, and in either case, need the correct instructions to make them as effective as possible and, most importantly, they need to work together.

Whatever the situation, the idea is for the two forwards to make the play of the opposing team predictable. In other words, attempt to force the opposing defenders to play the ball in a certain direction or to a certain area of the field. If the forwards can do this, it makes it easier for the midfielders and defenders to read and anticipate, and therefore more likely to force a turnover and regain possession.

Of course, any time a lively striker might be able to prey on an unsuspecting or tardy defender and exploit a situation for himself or his partner, possibly stealing the ball, is to be encouraged.

The easiest method to teach this would be using a tactics board or even pen and paper. When the ideas have been explained, the practical side should be implemented in a coached 11 v 11 game where play can be stopped and appropriate explanations given.

In this chapter we will cover all four options for the forwards; pressing against three and four defenders and playing deep against three and four defenders.

cp: Must make play predictable

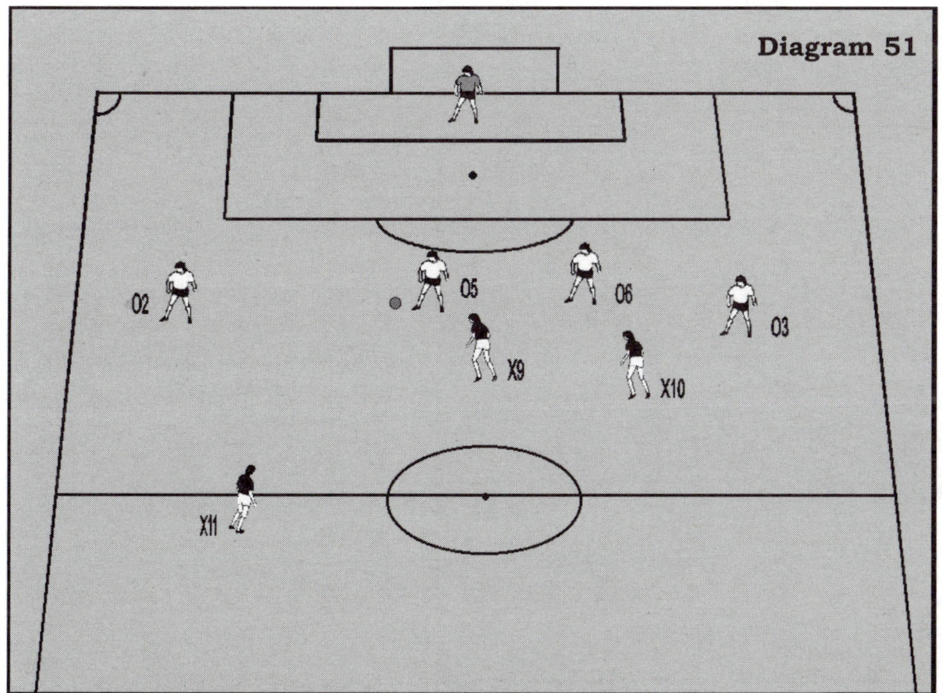

Diagram 51

Two Forwards Against a Back Four - Pressing

The first strategy that a coach might adopt is for the strikers to try to work the ball to one of the fullbacks. For instance, he might know the opposition has a fullback who may have a perceived weakness e.g. a poor kicker of the ball.

He can then set up the rest of the team to defend when the ball is with one of them.

So, in the diagram, we can see that O5 has possession.

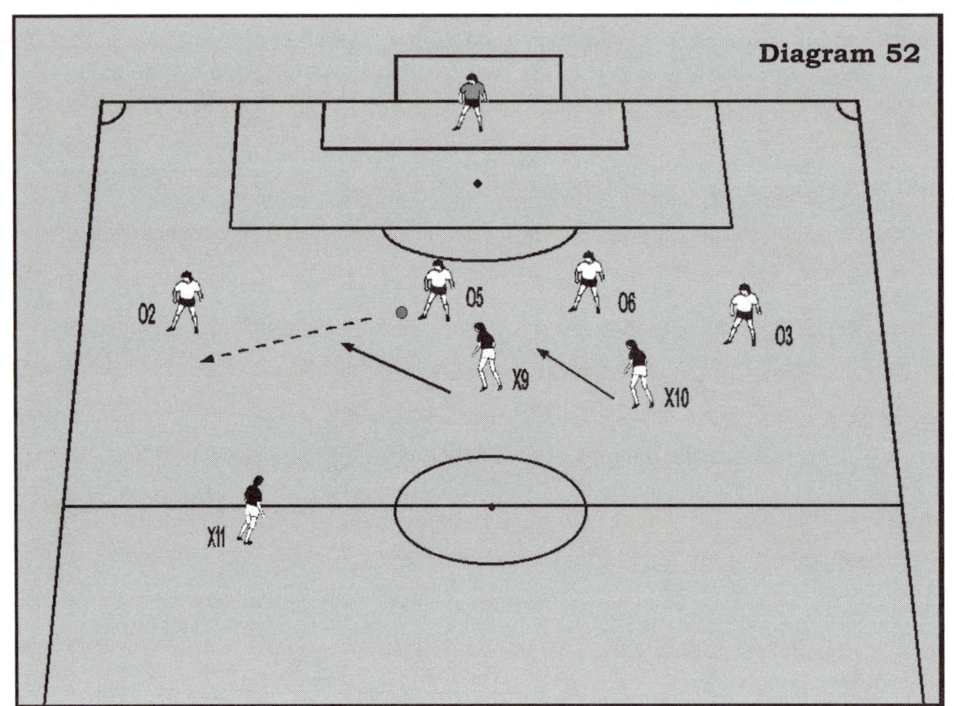

X9 allows O5 to pass to O2 and then moves to prevent O2 passing back to O5. This forces O2 to pass to a player on that side of the field, which is the objective.

X9 must then pressure O2 forcing him to make the pass up the field.

Defending OM can mark attacking OM then ~~pressure O2~~ forcing him to make ineffective pass down middle (i.e. OM has taken away pass to OM on attack & X9 pressures O2)

CP: MF should mark up tightly when the FW are making predictable

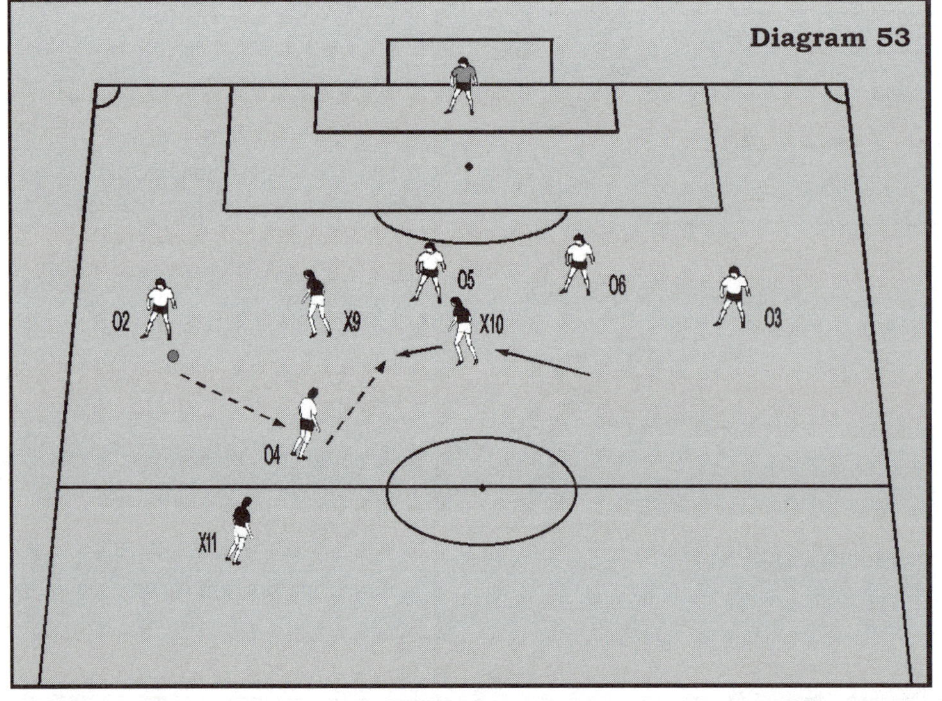

X10 must also slide over to prevent O2 from attempting to pass back to O5 or from O5 receiving a pass from a midfielder (O4).

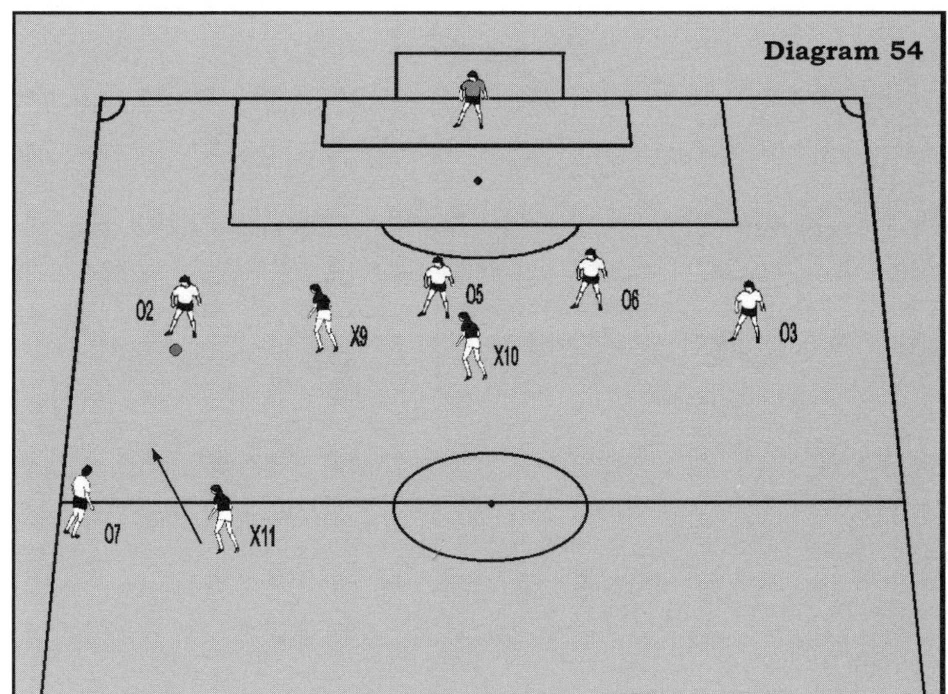

X11 moves to challenge O2 and prevent a pass to O7.

Thus, the options for O2 are reduced, there are no easy passes, all the X's are marking correctly and when O2 does release the ball, the X's have a good chance of regaining possession.

Remember, the work of the forwards will be wasted if the defenders and midfielders fail to support them.

A second plan could be to try to give the center backs possession of the ball and force the play through the middle. The forwards encourage the center backs to either play straight passes forward, which is easier for the defending team, or allow the center back to bring the ball forward. As soon as this happens,, the strikers apply a pincer movement. Such a ploy either makes O5 rush his pass or has him caught in possession.

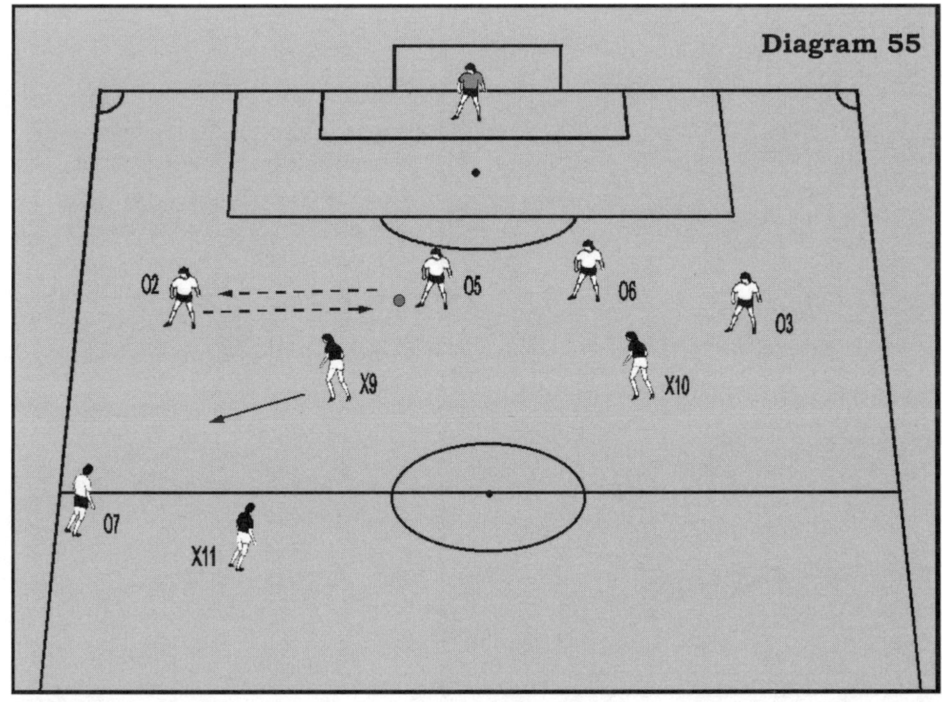

In this example, the ball is passed wide to O2. X9 then moves to prevent a pass up the flank and force the pass inside back to O5 again.

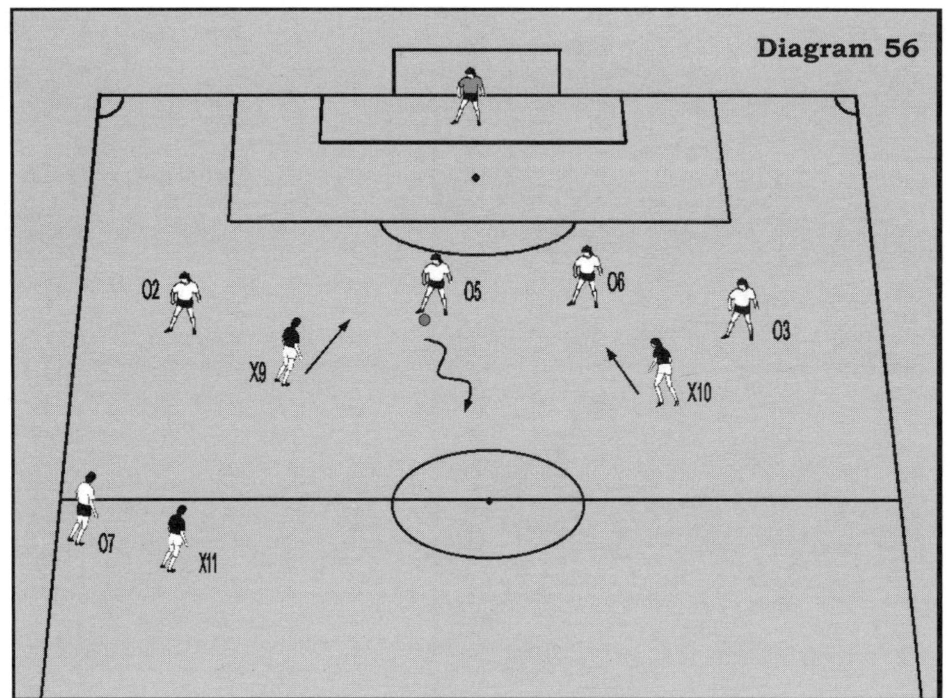

As soon as O5 receives the ball, X9 and X10 should position themselves outside of O5 and O6 and prevent passes to O2 and O3. They then apply a "pincer" movement by pressuring the ball from either side and forcing 05 to play up the middle.

In both these instances, it may not be the strikers who directly win the ball. What they do achieve however, are limited options for the player in possession and this greatly assists team defending.

Two Forwards Against a Back Three - Pressing

Two strikers against three defenders initially seems like better odds than 2 v 4. However, in such circumstances the defending team are now likely to be outnumbered in midfield. Therefore, some thought must be given to how the forwards will defend to avoid their efforts being wasted and the ball being passed to an unmarked midfield opponent

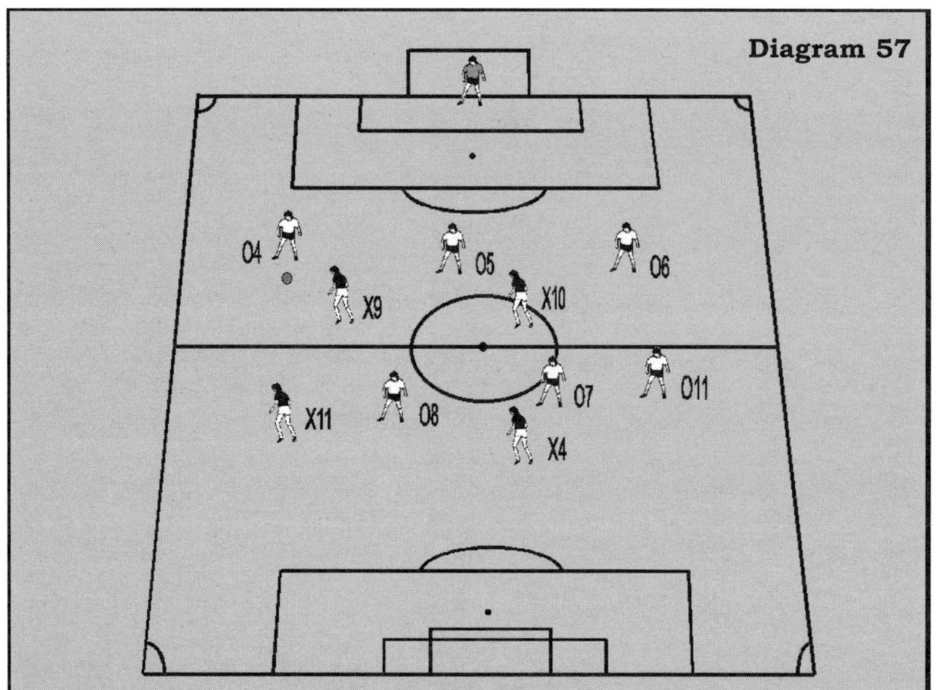

Again, if the coach is familiar with the opposition, he may instruct his strikers to 'allow' a particular player, (the perceived weakness) to have the ball. If this is not known before the game, then it is something that the coach or, better still, the forwards might identify early into the match.

Should this not be the case, then the coach sets up the team to understand how to defend whenever O4, O5 or O6 have the ball.

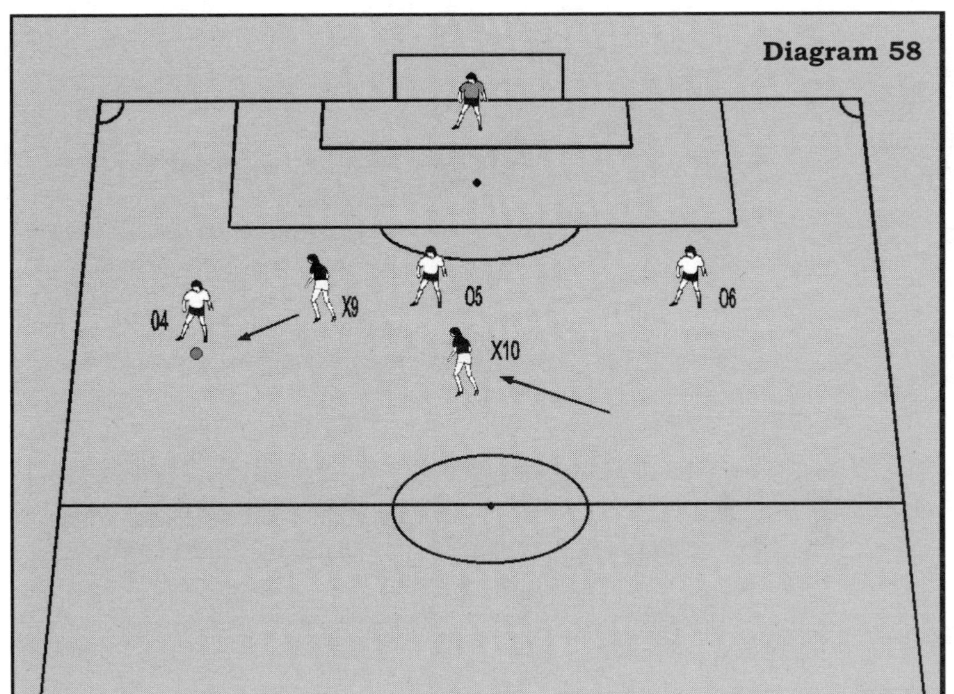

When O4 is in possession, X9 should press from the side and slightly behind to prevent O4 turning back. His partner, X10, moves across to mark O5. O6 is furthest from the ball and can be left unmarked as he is the least dangerous player.

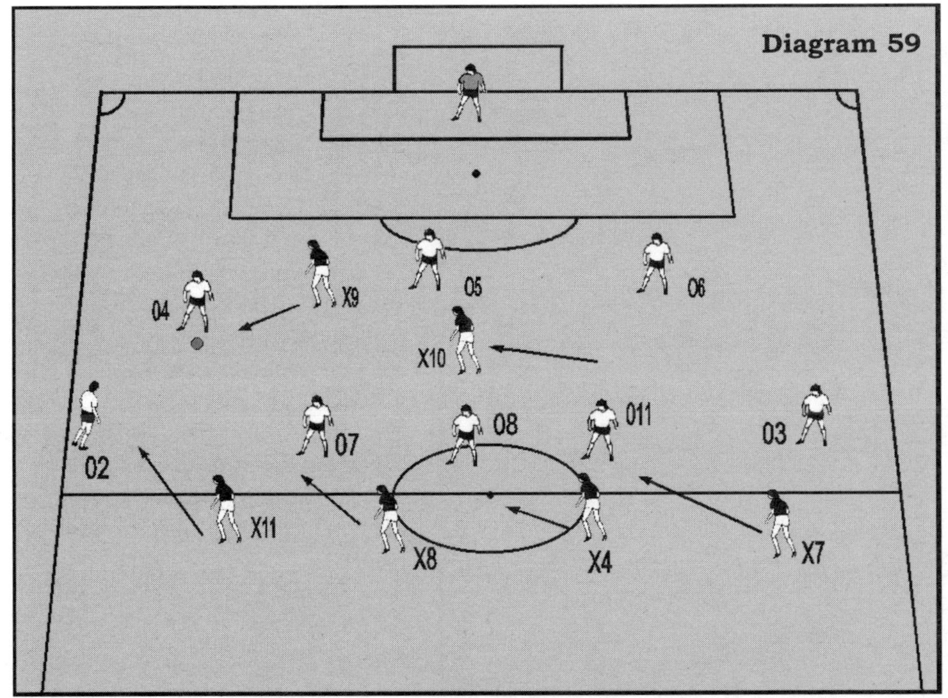

X11 closes on O2, X8 on O7 and X4 and X7 also slide across to minimize the space in midfield. O3 can be left unmarked as he is a long way from the ball and of least danger.

By the strikers doing their job, O4 has limited options and the X's have a good chance of regaining possession.

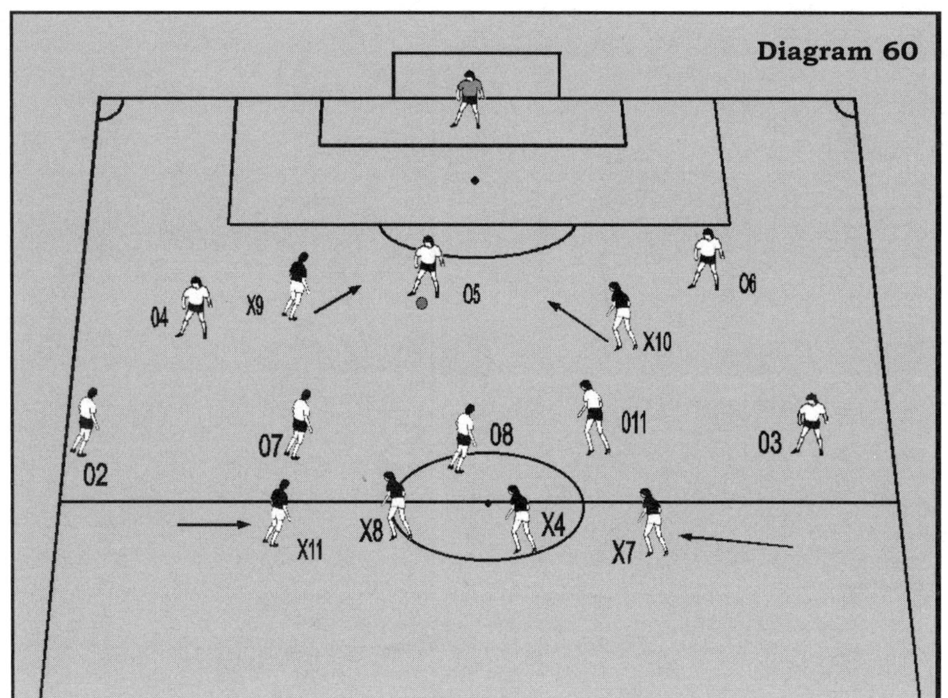

Where O5 has the ball and comes forward, the strikers again should apply the pincer movement. But there may be a problem in midfield where the O's have an extra player. In this situation the X midfield four must stay narrow to congest the area.

In doing so, it is likely that the ball will eventually be forced to O4 or O6 and the defending can follow the pattern outlined previously.

Two Forwards Against a Back Four - Deep

The coach who instructs his team to defend deep intends to concede ground to the opposition. The team allows just enough space behind his back four for the goalkeeper to sweep, and use the forwards to help condense the space between the back of his team and the front as shown below.

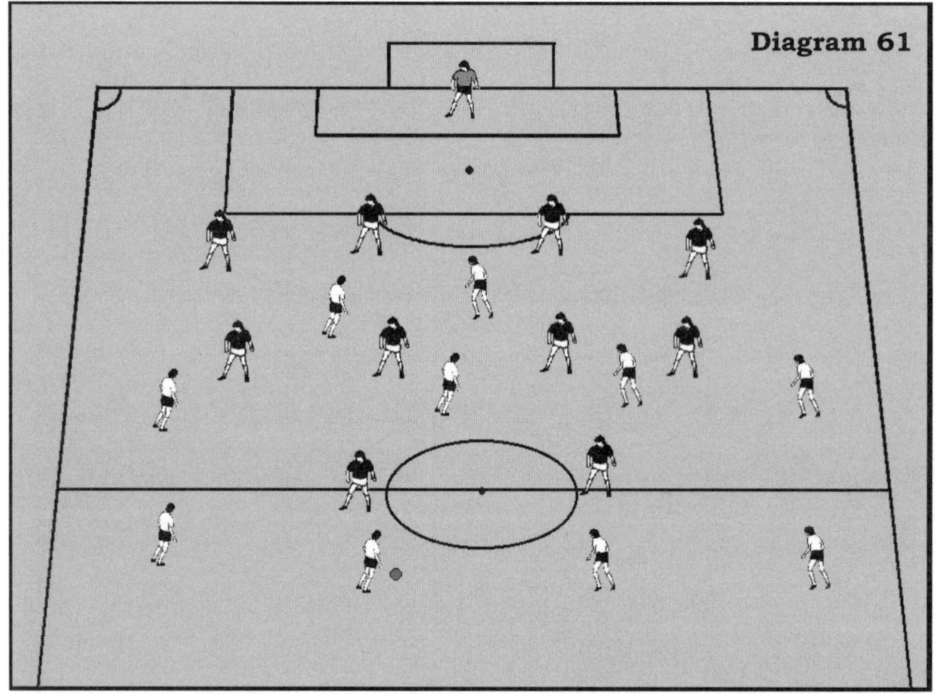

Such tactics should not deter the strikers to be on the lookout and ready to pounce on a misplaced pass or a poor piece of control from an opponent. If the forwards are able to steal the ball, the team should then look to launch a counter-attack as quickly as possible.

When the forwards don't steal the ball, the team withdraws and allows the opposition to play in front of them.

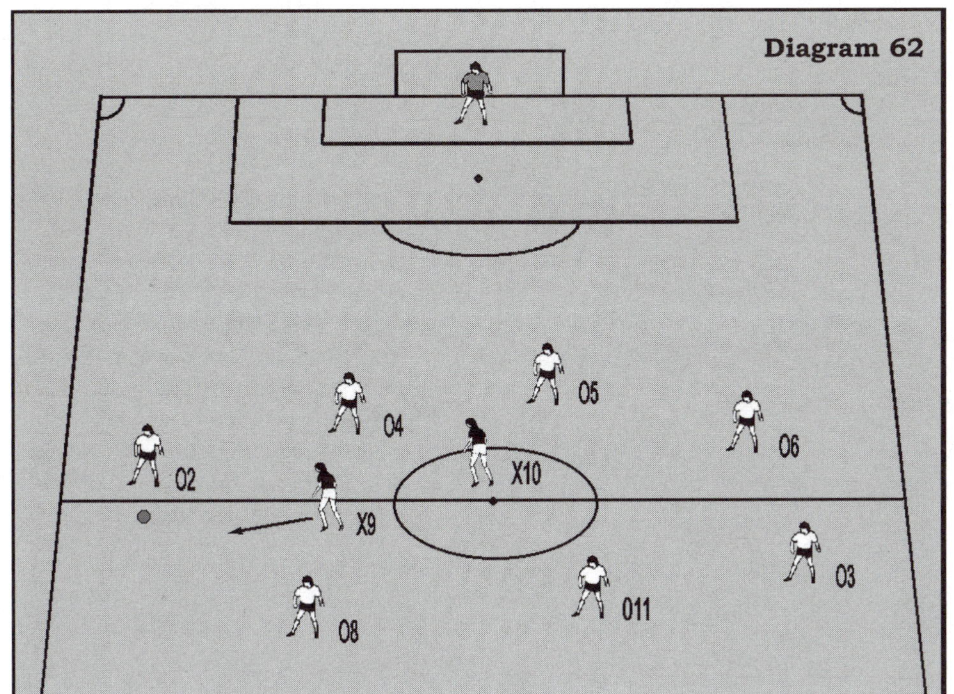

In this example, O2 has possession. X9 may not be able to close immediately but is edging closer. X10 has two roles to consider. First, to prevent a big change of play to O3, which could wrong foot the defence. Second, to limit the space of O8 and O11 to drop deep to receive the ball.

cp: Second FW should maintain good distance (ie. around middle of field) because if he moves over to close to X9 he leaves team vulnerable to Δ of point of attack to O3. Since CD will drop back, if FW in middle wins ball there's plenty of room for counter.

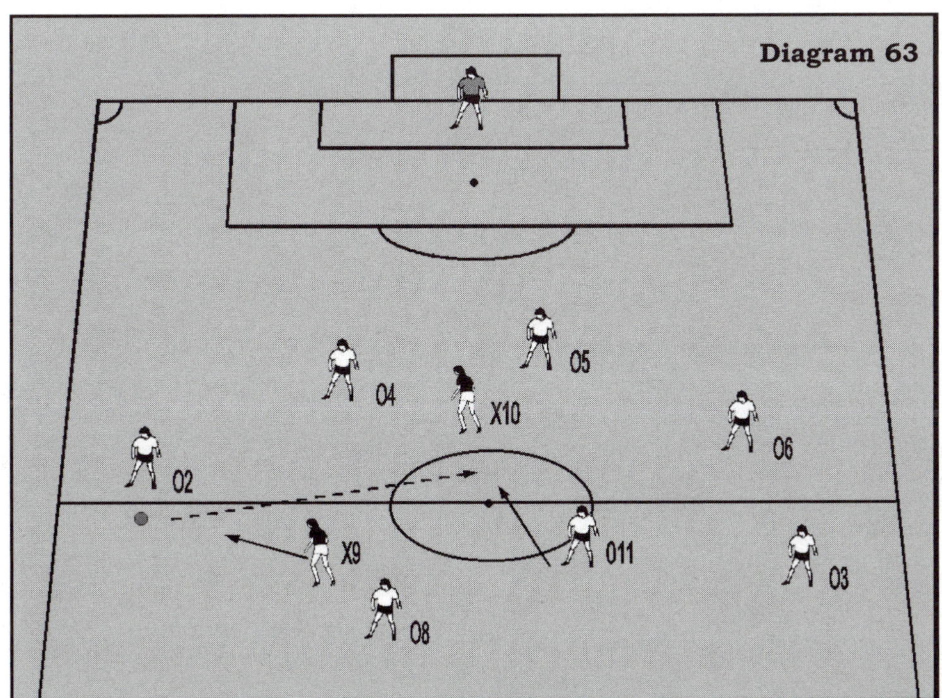

Limiting the opportunities for 08 and 011 to drop back and receive the ball is a point that can easily be missed.

If X10 chooses to stay too high, as shown, the space available in midfield increases. O8 and O11 are happy to receive the ball knowing where the markers are.

So X10 should fill in a little deeper so that 08 and 011 have less space to receive the ball.

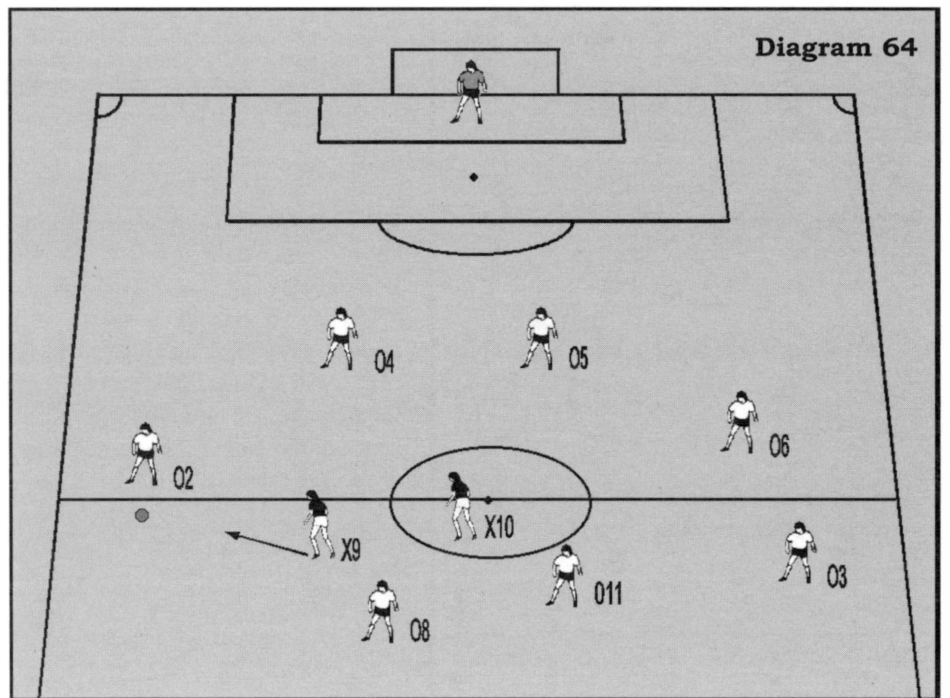

There is also something else to be gained for X10 in taking up this position. You will notice that O4 and O5 have dropped deep to make themselves available to O2. This leaves X10 unmarked. So an intercepted pass by the midfield players or a headed clearance by a center back, puts him in an ideal position to take possession, turn and start a counter-attack.

Two Forwards Against Three Defenders - Deep

The work of the strikers against a back three is very similar. What they now have to consider are the demands of the midfield behind. X7 has to come in-field to help even numbers up centrally. This means the change of play is a big advantage for the opposition and needs to be avoided.

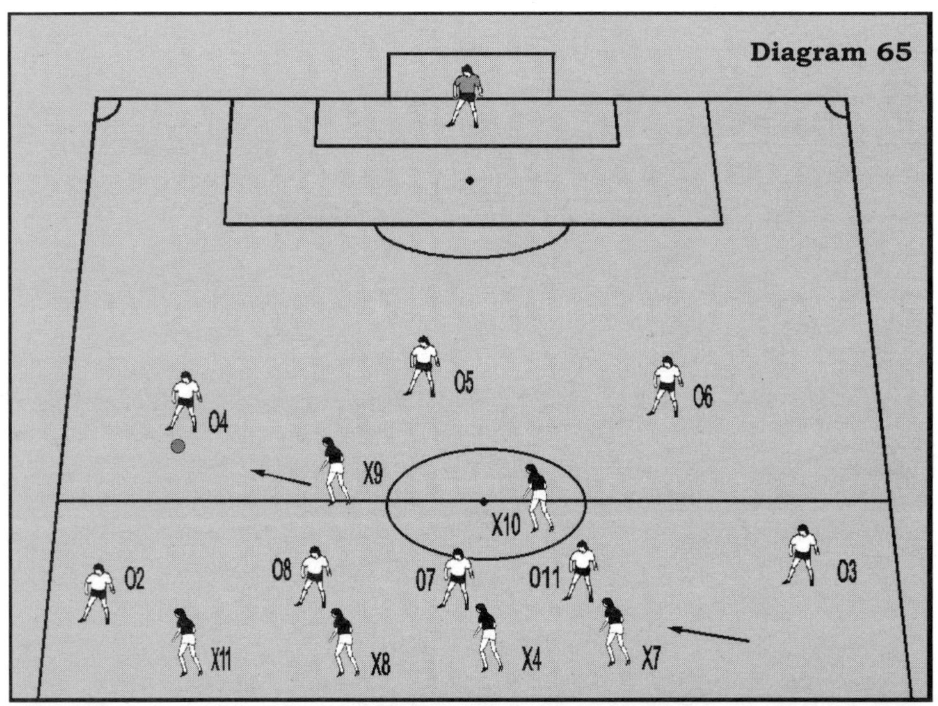

This time X9 and X10 help prevent this by X10 not going too far across the pitch.

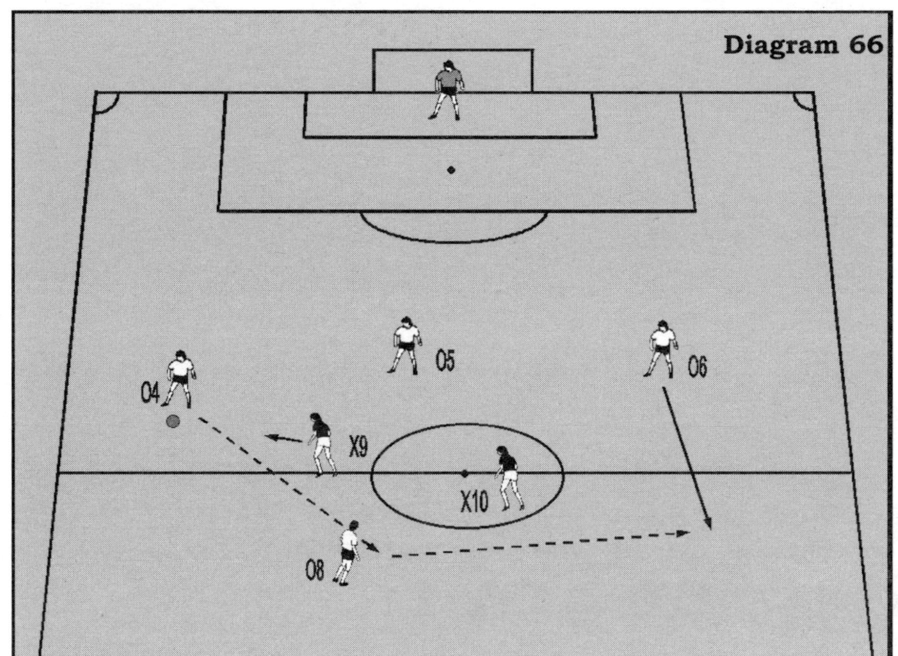

X10 needs to play as deep as before but not allow O6 to slip too far away so that a pass from O4 to O6 either directly or though a midfield player, changes the point of the attack.

As you can see there is a bonus for X10 this time and that any change of possession which comes to him means one less defender between him and the goal.

Conclusion

Although the forwards operate the furthest from their own goal, they still have an important part to play in the team's defending. In fact, one challenge for the coach is to make the team understand how to play WITHOUT the ball and that includes the strikers. The forwards should still be defending when the ball is past them and in and around their own penalty box.

If a center back is brave enough to challenge for a ball in the air and head it clear or a midfield player prepared to block a thunderbolt of a shot, they would like to know that the clearance or the rebound might possibly drop to a striker who is not spectating but reading the play and ready to take possession and prevent it going back towards his own goal.

And what about the time when a misdirected cross is collected by the goalkeeper? Are the strikers ready to take advantage of the situation and initiate a counter attack?

The examples we have looked at are all set piece situations, and of course soccer is not like that all the time. However, the practices and examples shown, if practiced often enough, will lead to players that know their responsibilities and can make it difficult for the other team and not allow them to get into a rhythm.

English Premier League Comparisons

The majority of top teams play with a retreating defence. This has evolved because of the improved skill level of defenders. At the top level, all players in all positions are comfortable in possession. Consequently, the tactic of pressing on every occasion becomes futile because the defenders just pass through the advancing team. Forwards have also become so quick that a team pressing is vulnerable to pacey forwards utilizing the space behind the back line.

Liverpool rarely press, unless, like most others they recognize a technical weakness in the opposition defenders. They are also aware that in their own strikers, especially Michael Owen, have pace that can hurt the opposition in a counter-attack.

Only when playing in the European Champions league do Arsenal and Manchester United show any variations in their defending. In the English Premier League, both teams enjoy so much possession that they rarely have to make special provision in their defensive strategy. Mostly it is a simple philosophy of once possession is lost "get back behind the ball".

When playing in Europe, and especially away from home, a cautious, defend deep strategy is employed and the strikers follow the defensive positions described.

What is very noticeable, is that strikers of all three clubs (Owen, Heskey, Van Nistelrooy, Solskjaer, Henry and Bergkamp) work extremely hard for the team defensively.

Chapter Four

Attacking With The Back Four

All the great teams expect every player to be able to play a part in the attacking potency of the team. Even the role of the goalkeeper, a position we have not analyzed, has to play his part.

In the days when Schmeichel was in his prime at Manchester United, the opposition always needed to be on guard when he claimed possession of the ball. Often when he was able to collect a poorly hit cross, in an instant, he was able to hurl the ball 40 yards or more to a sprinting Giggs on the left or to Kanchelsikis, the Russian, on the right and a counter-attack was begun.

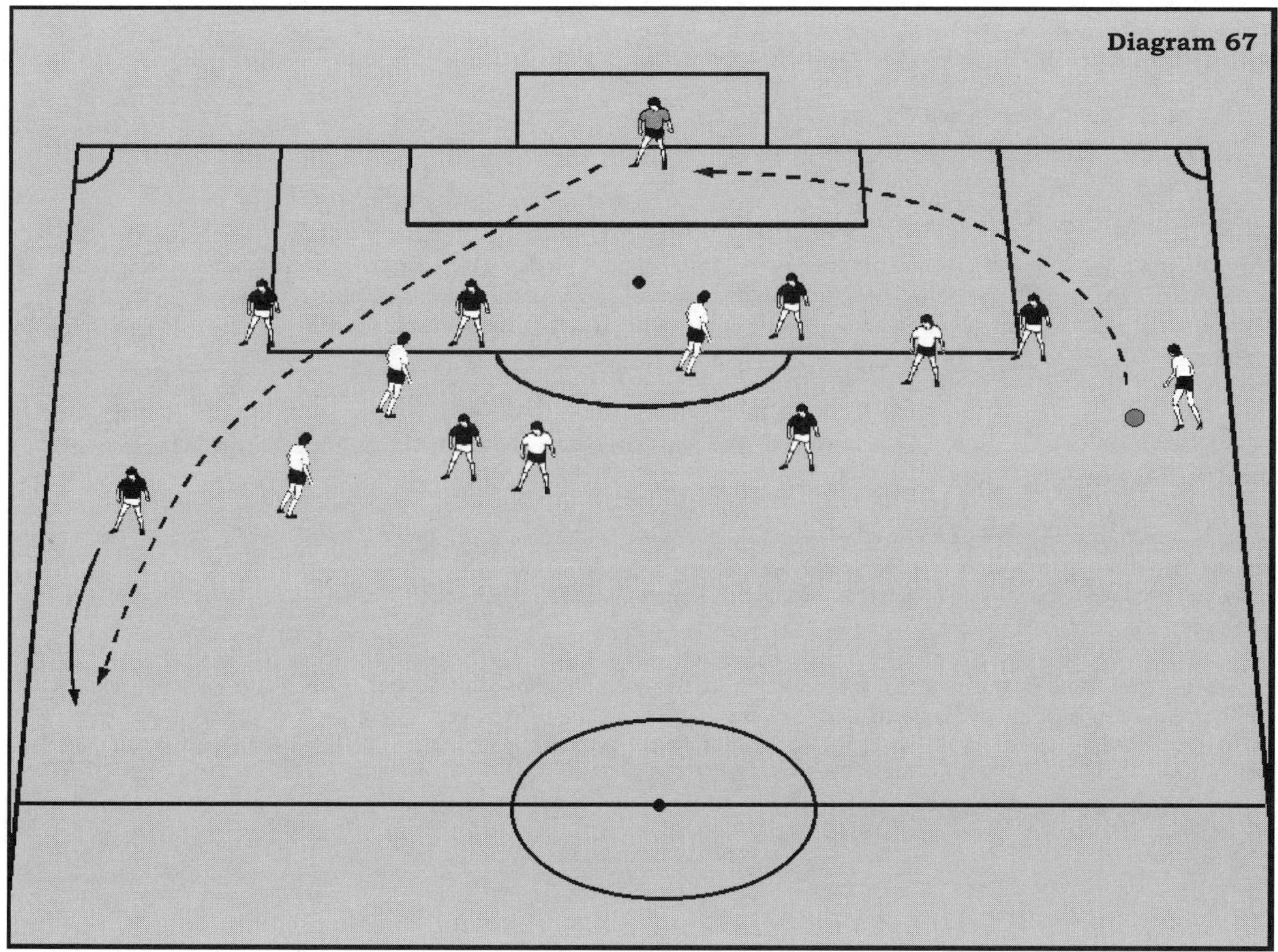

On numerous occasions, Schmeichel's awareness and skill at finding the raiding player produced goals and goal scoring opportunities for Manchester United. Where Schmeichel led, others followed, and other coaches demanded the same degree of awareness from their own goalkeepers.

This tradition at Old Trafford has now been followed by the eccentric French World Cup winner, Fabien Barthez who has taken things to another level. Not only is his throwing in the same class as Schmeichel's, but his kicking poses an equal threat.

The glamorous players in the great teams are usually the strikers, but they rely heavily on those who help create the chances by which they score the goals that make their reputations. So the next stage is to look at the role of the back and midfield four in attacking situations and then finally the strikers themselves.

In order to be effective in starting or helping attacks, defenders need to be comfortable in possession of the ball. Although the center backs don't need to be skillful dribblers, they need to be able to make themselves available to receive the ball and then select good passing options to retain possession.

This is really a minimum requirement in the modern game. At the top level, center backs are now expected to be able to hit long and short passes as well as take advantage of space in front of them by stepping forward with the ball or sometimes without it.

Defending is still their priority, and they must always know where their man is so that on a change of possession they are not caught out of position. However, simply standing next to an opponent when your team is attacking is not good enough. Defenders have to read the game and have two things in mind.

(1) Where do I need to be if required to receive a pass?
(2) Where do I need to be if we lose possession?

This requires excellent concentration because any lapse will be exploited by an opponent.

Apart from the goalkeeper, the center backs in a 4-4-2 formation are probably the only two players who rarely change position. They may of course, through the flow of the game, find themselves on a flank or stepping into midfield. But as part of the attacking strategy of the team they are not usually involved in any interchanges that might try to outwit the opposition.

It is, however, different with the fullbacks. They can be effectively employed to do damage to the opposition. Earlier, we looked at Ashley Cole of Arsenal and his attacking qualities. The coach who has fullbacks of this calibre at his disposal needs to take advantage of them.

Cole is able to dribble and beat players, but not all fullbacks are this versatile. At the very least though, the coach should expect his fullbacks to have the desire to get into advanced positions through hard but intelligent running. Once there, they need to be able to cross the ball in a variety of ways. A long high cross beyond the far post, a curling under hit delivery to the near post, low driven crosses, etc.

In order to give some idea on how this may be achieved, consider the following practices. Note that in each one, the fullback is dependant upon the understanding he has with his wide midfield player. Consequently, we have the reverse of a defending situation where the wide midfielder and fullback worked together to prevent threatening moves from the opposition.

Attacking With The Fullbacks

This practice takes the form of a drill to explain the interchange between the fullback and wide midfielder. It can also be used as a *"finishing from crosses"* practice for the strikers as well.

By doubling up in some of the positions, and setting up players on the left flank, it is possible to get a continuous practice. Conditions can also be put on the fullbacks to deliver certain types of crosses and also to players in the box to fill certain areas. For example, the near and far post spaces must be filled.

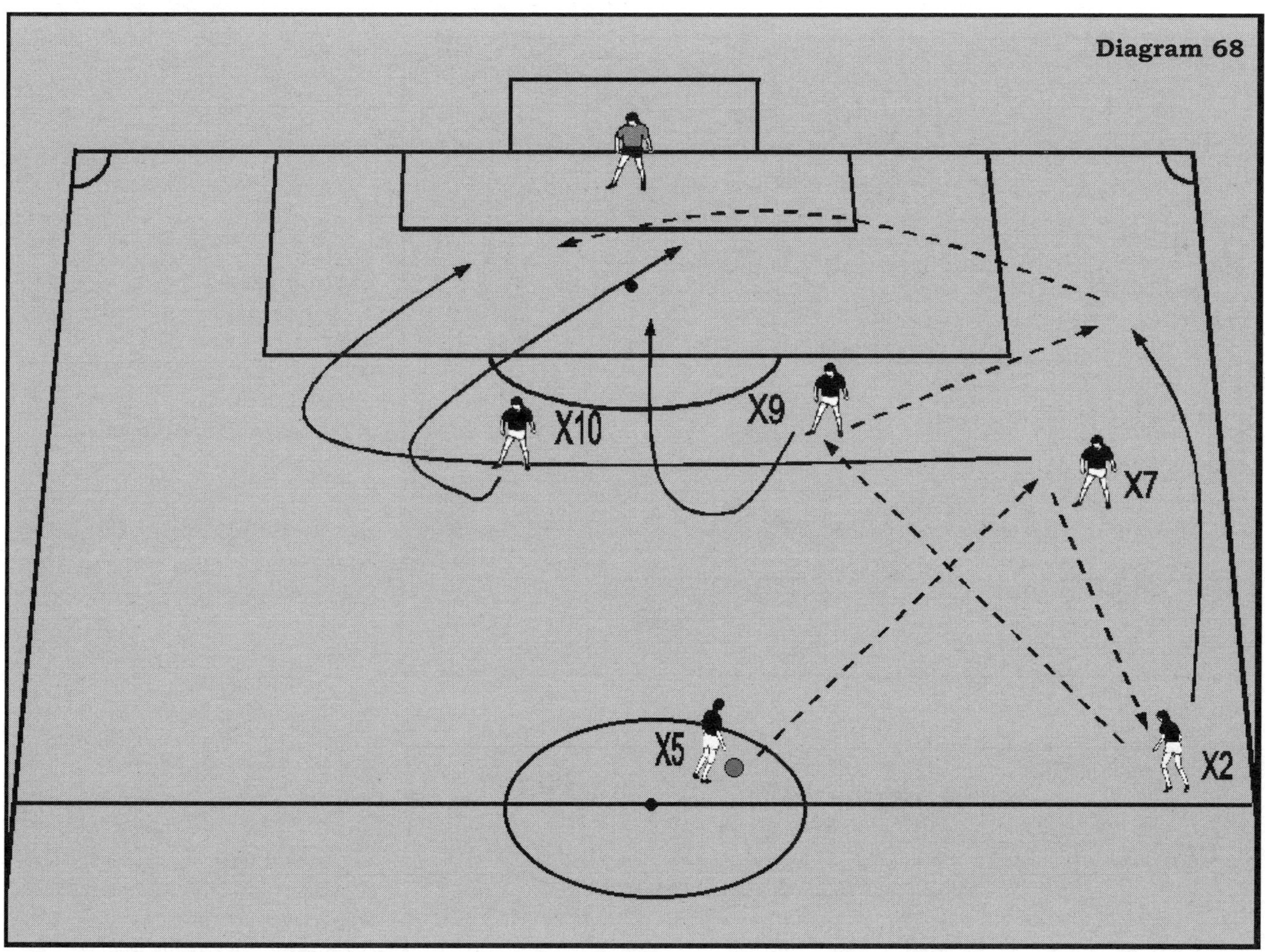

X5 passes wide to X7.
X7 sets the ball back for X2 (fullback).
X7 runs inside and across X9.
X2 passes to X9 and makes an overlapping run.
X9 passes wide for overlapping X2 who crosses.
X7 and X10 make far and near post runs respectively.
X9 spins and makes a run to the center of the penalty area.

Attacking With The Fullbacks - Two

The following rotations are practiced unopposed. However, it should be noted that by coming toward the ball in a game situation, X7 poses a dilemma for his marker. Should he follow X7 or should he be more concerned about the forward run of X2? Option one assumes that the marker follows X7. Option two is where X7 gets away from his marker.

This practice is something the coach needs to explain by firstly walking through the movements. Having all the players involved understand the timing of their runs is vital. Although the 'best' pass is to the overlapping full back X2, X5 also needs to be aware that X7 coming short, unmarked and turning is also an option.

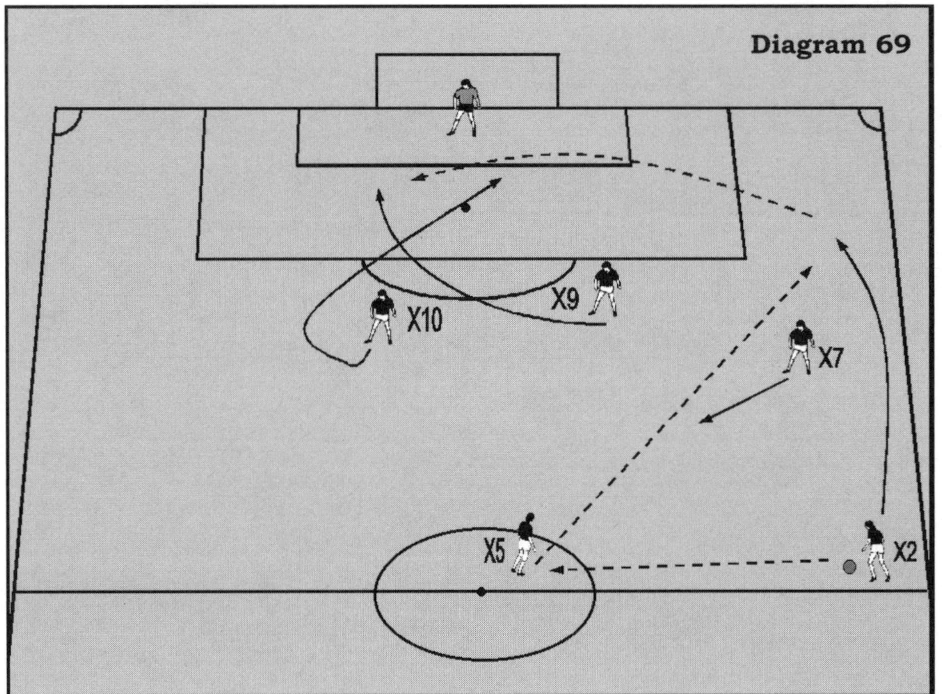

Option One

X2 passes inside to X5 and makes an overlapping run.
X7 makes a run inside to make space for X2's run.
X5 passes wide to overlapping X2.

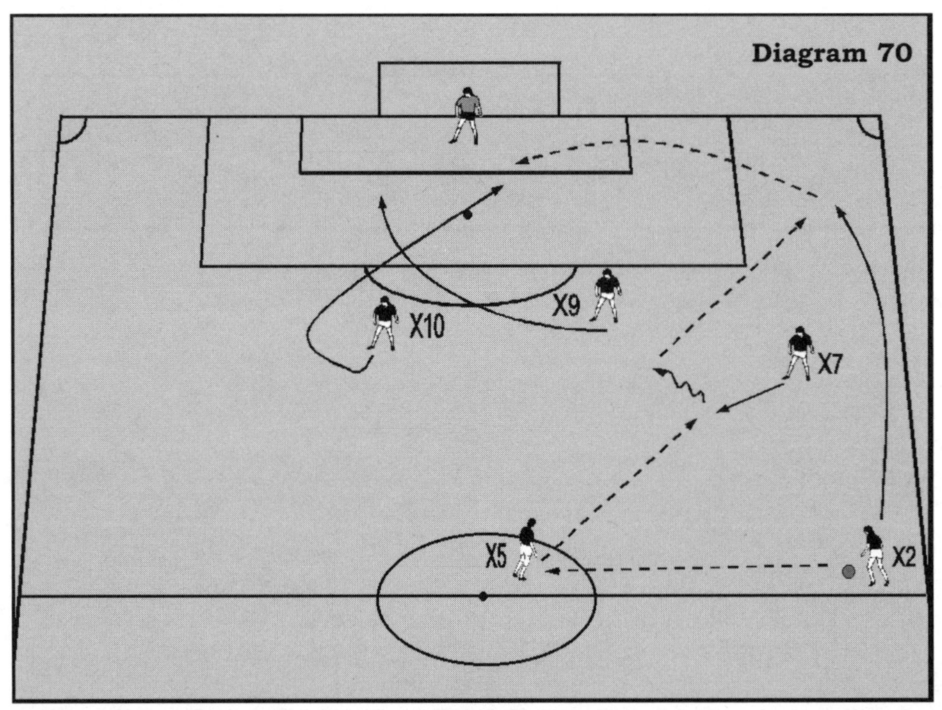

Option Two

X2 passes inside to X5 and makes an overlapping run.
X7 makes a run inside to make space for X2's run.
If X7 is free and has space, X5 passes to him. X7 then turns inside with the ball.

For the purposes of the exercise, X7 would play wide to X2 to deliver the cross. However, in a game situation, X7 would also need to be aware of how to penetrate using X9 and X10.

Attacking With The Fullbacks - Three

In this rotation, the midfielder involved (X8) needs to have time on the ball in order for X7 to make a threatening run inside and X2 to move forward into the vacated space. Again, a clear explanation is required initially making certain all players involved understand their role.

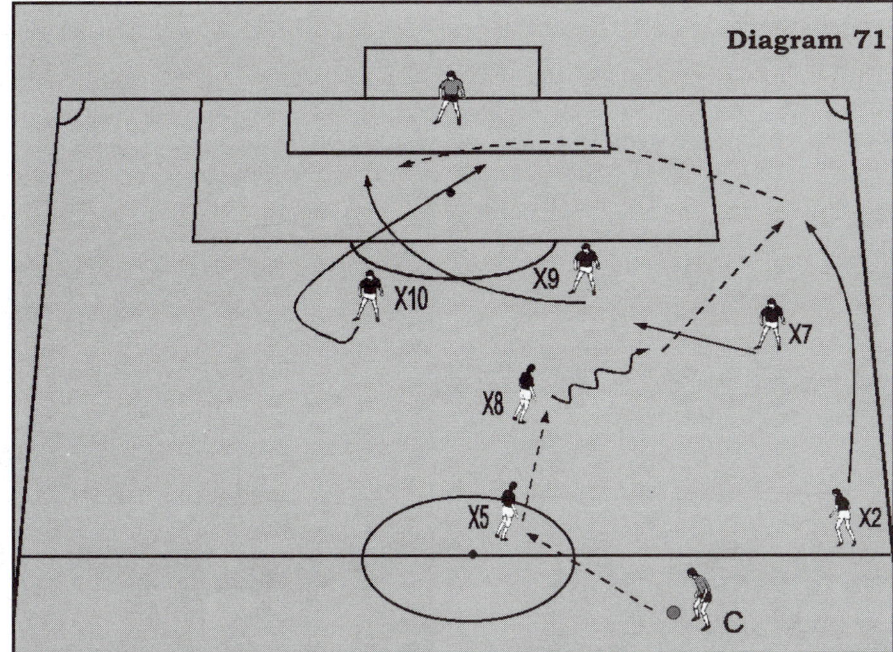

The coach passes to X5.
X5 passes into the midfielder, X8.
X7 makes an attacking run inside.
X8 attacks the space and passes to the overlapping X2.

Diagram 72

Having established the preceding options in the players minds, it now needs to be translated into a match practice or small-sided game. For example, a 9 v 9 game (8 v 8 plus GKs) on a shortened field as shown. The teams should be organized in a 3-3-2 formation.

The next step would be to move to an 11 v 11 game on a full field.

This is an ideal formation for practicing in an opposed situation what has been learned before. One center defender and one center midfielder should be used. This lends itself to combination play between the fullbacks and wide midfielders.

Focus on one team and stop the game occasionally to point out instances where players haven't recognized the situations that were rehearsed earlier. Be careful not to manufacture situations, allow them to occur naturally within the course of the game. And of course, always encourage successful and especially new combinations that the players create themselves.

Chapter Five

Attacking With The Midfield Four

Attacking With The Wide Midfielders

The scope in attacking plays and ideas from the midfielders depends very much on the individual ability of the players at the coach's disposal. For example, Liverpool do not possess a player like Manchester United's Ryan Giggs who is an excellent dribbler. The asset of a player like Giggs can play a major part in how a team attacks.

However, what is possible is to encourage movement, either individually or collectively, in order to cause maximum disruption to the opposition. In this, we have already looked at how the fullback and wide midfielder might combine. In the following roles and diagrams are some ideas of other combinations involving the wide players and then the central midfield duo.

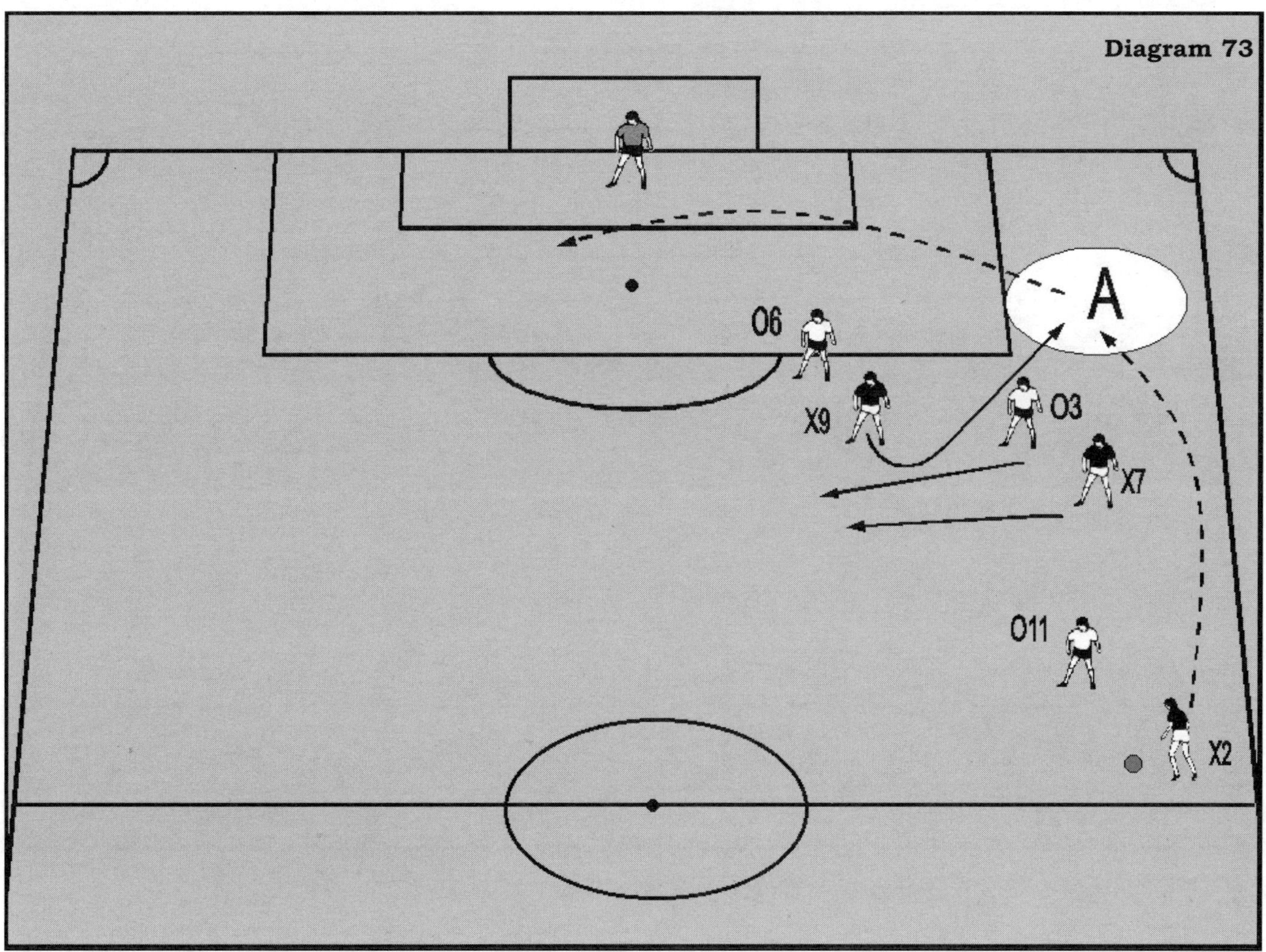

In this situation where X2 has the ball, X7 has a decision to make in trying to help. If he stays where he is, then he would receive the ball with O3 marking tight and O11 ready to chase back. If he runs inside, he leaves space A for the forward, X9 to exploit.

This next example is one that Arsenal's wide midfield players are excellent at. Pires, Ljungberg and Wiltord all recognize the situation as it is developing and time their movement to perfection.

The trigger is often as in the diagram below where a forward is able to come deep, receive a pass and turn to face the opposing back line.

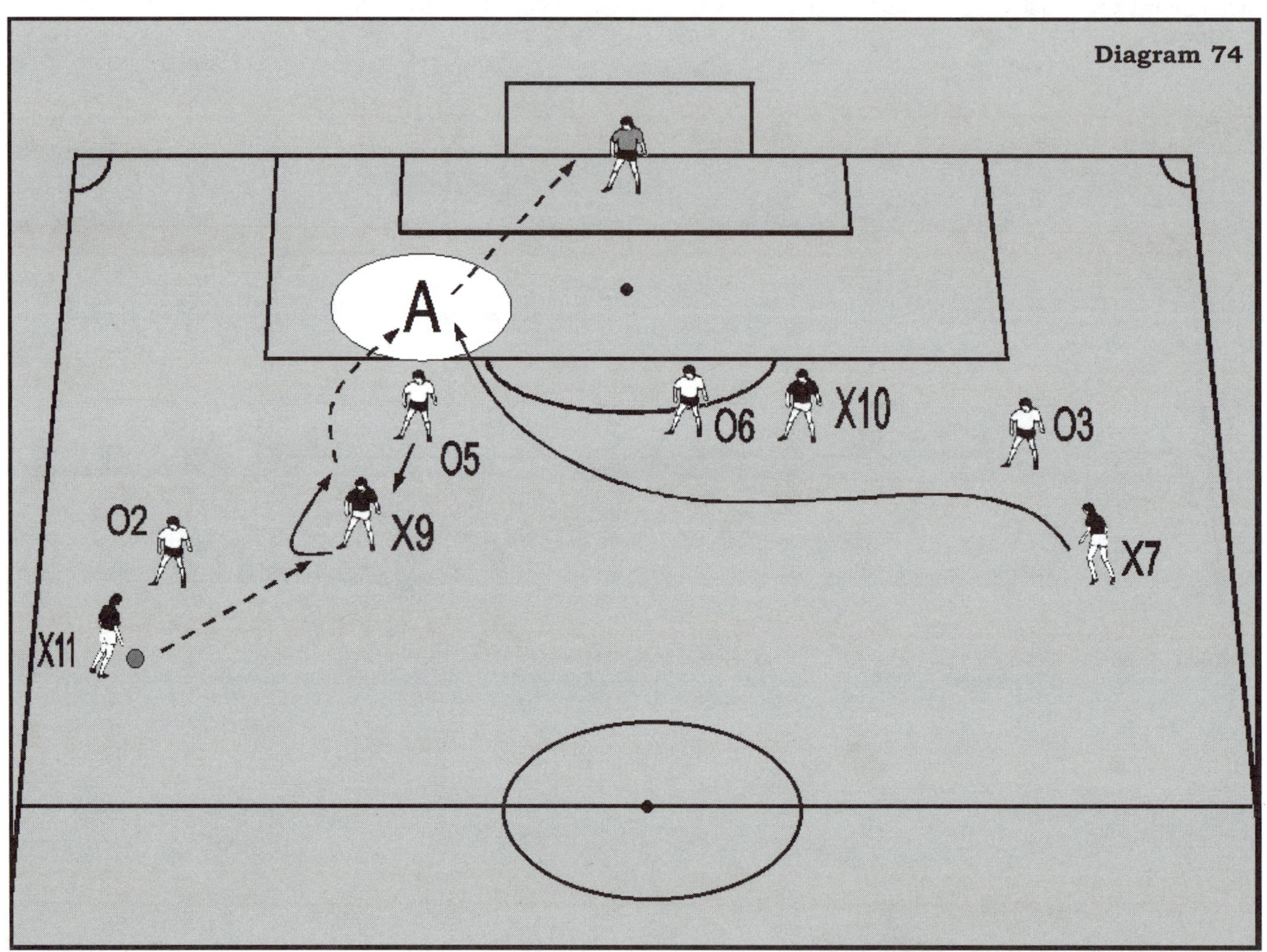

In this example, X9 comes deep to show for the ball, receives it and is able to turn and face the opposing defenders.

Before X9 even receives the ball, X7 has recognized the situation and starts to move, making a 'flat run' across the field.

The next decision is the timing of the run through the 'line of offside'. Go too soon, before the pass can be played and the run will be halted by the linesman's flag. Go too late, and O6 will have read the run and might get to the ball first.

This example is the sort of situation Manchester United winger, Ryan Giggs, with his pace often exploits.

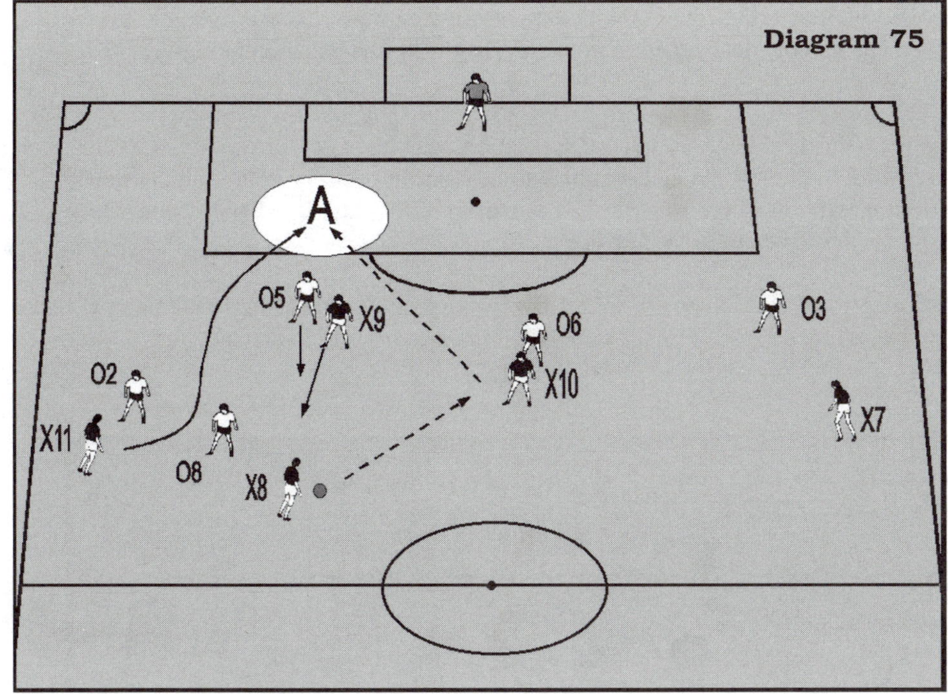

X9 comes short to try to dislocate the opposition back line. O5 has had to follow X9 to mark tightly but this leaves space A available to exploit. Very often O2 and O6 are aware of the danger too late. O2 might relax because O8 is forcing X8 to play inside. X11 can take advantage of this when X8 passes inside for X10 who passes quickly into space A for X11.

The pass into X10 and from X10 can be achieved even if X10 is marked tightly.

These are just a few ideas and by sowing the seeds of one or two basic interchanges the coach can often stimulate ideas amongst the players.

By observing his own players, the coach can assess their individual strengths and how they can be used to maximum effect. From a coaching point of view, playing the small sided 3-3-2 game as described with the attacking fullbacks, is a good teaching format. Keep it simple and focus on just a couple of combinations initially rather than swamp the players with too many ideas.

English Premier League Comparisons

At Manchester United, Giggs' opposite number is England captain, David Beckham. His strength is not his dribbling ability but his passing, movement and especially his crossing of the ball. Beckham doesn't need to get beyond his marker to cross dangerously. Given just half a yard, Beckham can deliver a variety of lethal crosses that invite strikers to make contact and score.

At Liverpool, another England international, Danny Murphy, operates on the right flank. Like the Arsenal wide men, he can often be found in central attacking areas, unmarked and looking to get in behind opposition center backs. He has a good understanding with his England teammate Steven Gerrard, who automatically fills the hole left when Murphy goes on his forward raids.

Attacking With The Center Midfielders

How much attacking freedom does the coach allow his central midfield players? It depends on the characteristics of the players involved. For instance, is it part of their strength to go forward and create and score goals, or are they more suited to a defensive role, which allows their partner in the central midfield to go forward more. This is certainly true at Liverpool, where, as was described earlier, Hamann is more suited to protecting his back line which in turn gives Steven Gerrard more freedom to get forward.

Where a team has the luxury of two players, both capable of hurting the opposition when they get forward, then a balance needs to be struck. The coach needs his central midfielders to understand that they put the security of the team at risk if they both venture forward and out of position at the same time. Therefore, one needs to hold back, when the other goes forward and they need to be able to recognize these situations as they occur.

So when the team is able to work the ball into good crossing positions, the coach is expecting one central midfielder to be in the penalty area trying to score, while his partner supports around the edge of the penalty area anticipating any knock downs.

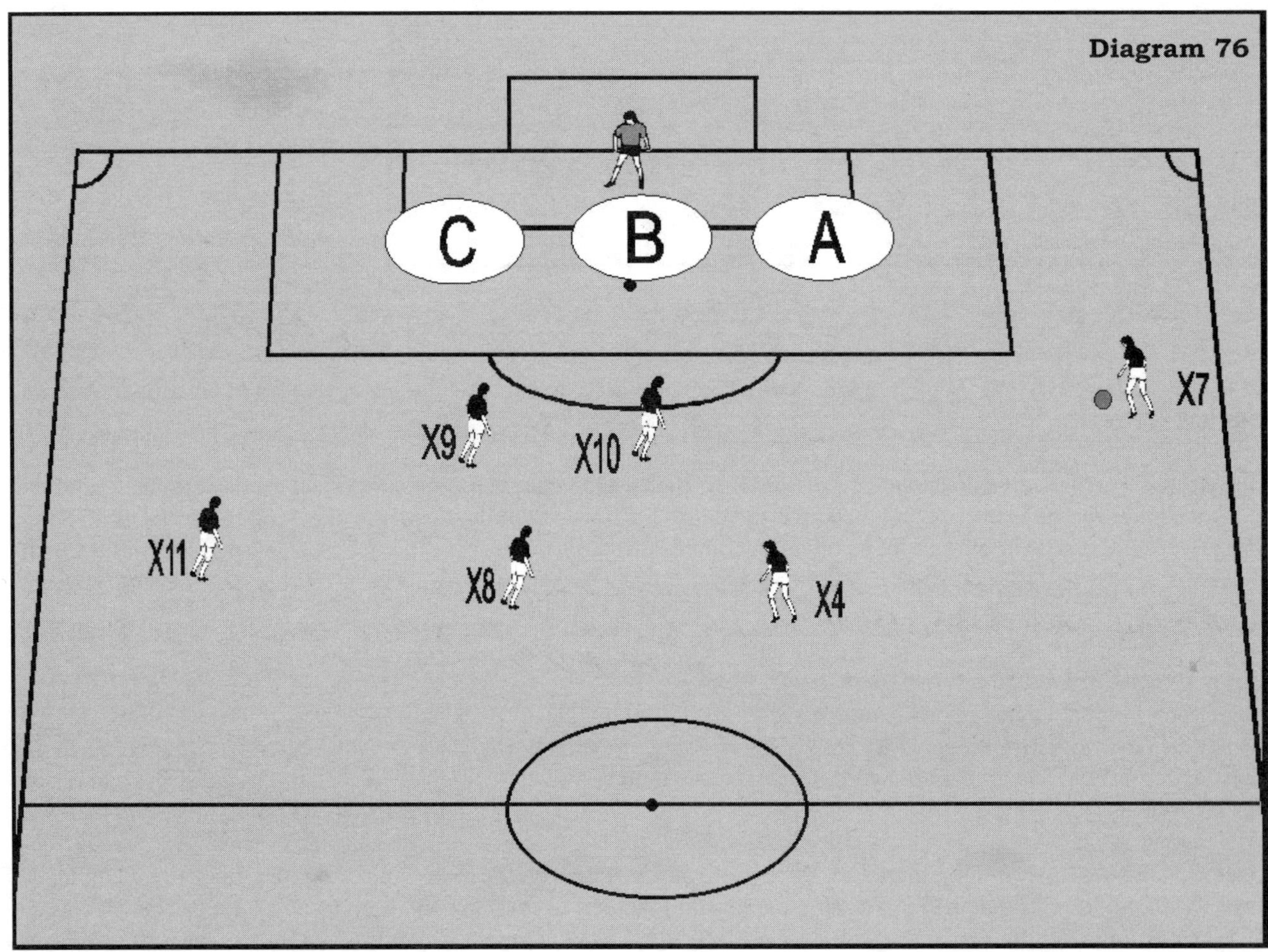

A, B and C refer to the three main areas that need to be filled when X7 gets into the crossing position shown. Obviously this requires a minimum of three attacking players and one would normally expect the two strikers (X9 and X10) to be involved. This means one more player is needed, which is usually one of the central midfielders (X8 or X4).

Of course there are occasions when it is impossible to expect this to happen and other occasions when X11 will be in a better position to get into the penalty area first. At such times, a decision has to be made by X8 and X4 as to whether or not to go into the box or stay outside looking for any knock downs. It should not be forgotten that this is also a goal scoring position. Any ball that drops free around the edge of the box can be seized upon and struck towards goal. Consequently good central midfield players need the confidence and technical ability to shoot from here.

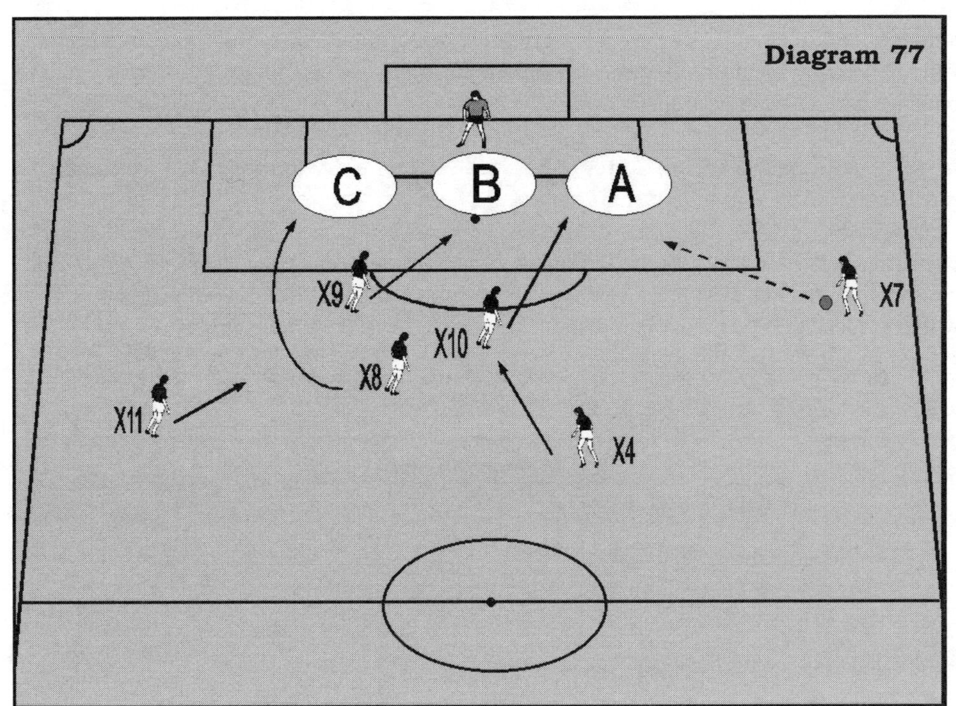

Option One

X8 is able to attack the far post position, so X11 and X4 hold positions outside of the penalty area looking for any knock downs.

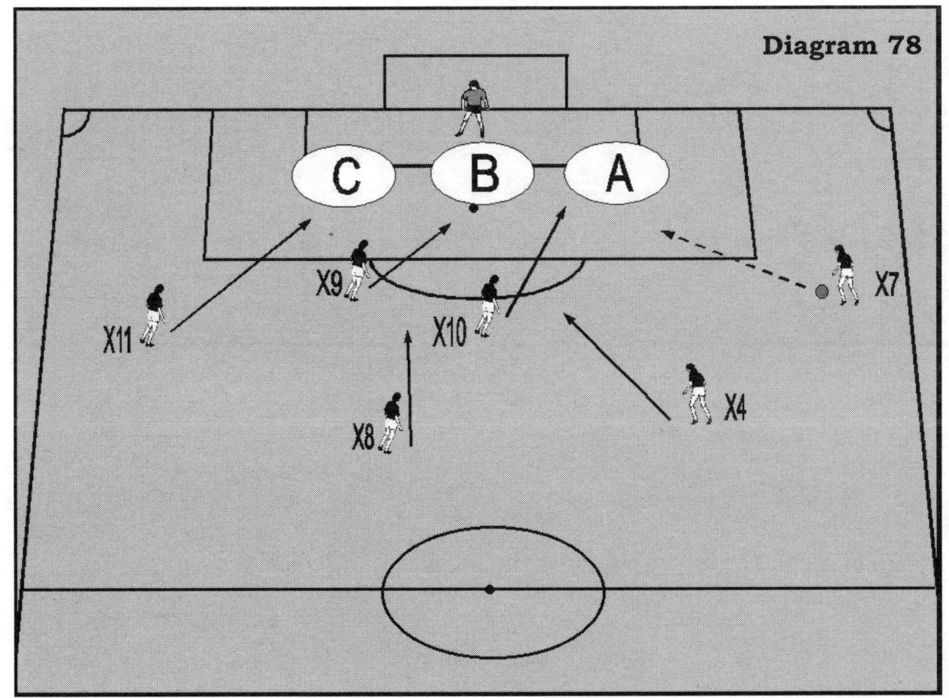

Option Two

X11 is able to get into an attacking position before X8. X8 and X4 should recognize this and hold their position outside the penalty area.

In the modern game most midfielders have excellent running power. This gives the opportunity for midfielders to exploit the space created by the movement of the strikers. Especially in games where the midfield area is congested, strong powerful runs behind the opposition back line are to be encouraged.

In the diagram below, X2 has possession, X9 has drawn O6 short and X10 has pulled away to try to move O5. Providing X2 can now deliver a quality pass, X8 needs to think about a hard run to attack space A.

Such a move tests the determination of his marker O4, as well as the defensive organization of the opposition. What should be remembered is that providing the pass from X2 is not over hit, any defender getting to the ball first may be forced to concede a throw-in. This would allow the X's to retain possession and start their next attack from the set play.

NB: In video X 8 is on left center of circle on attacking side of field
And Play starts with A different CM passing to X2. There is 4th defender on Right of circle

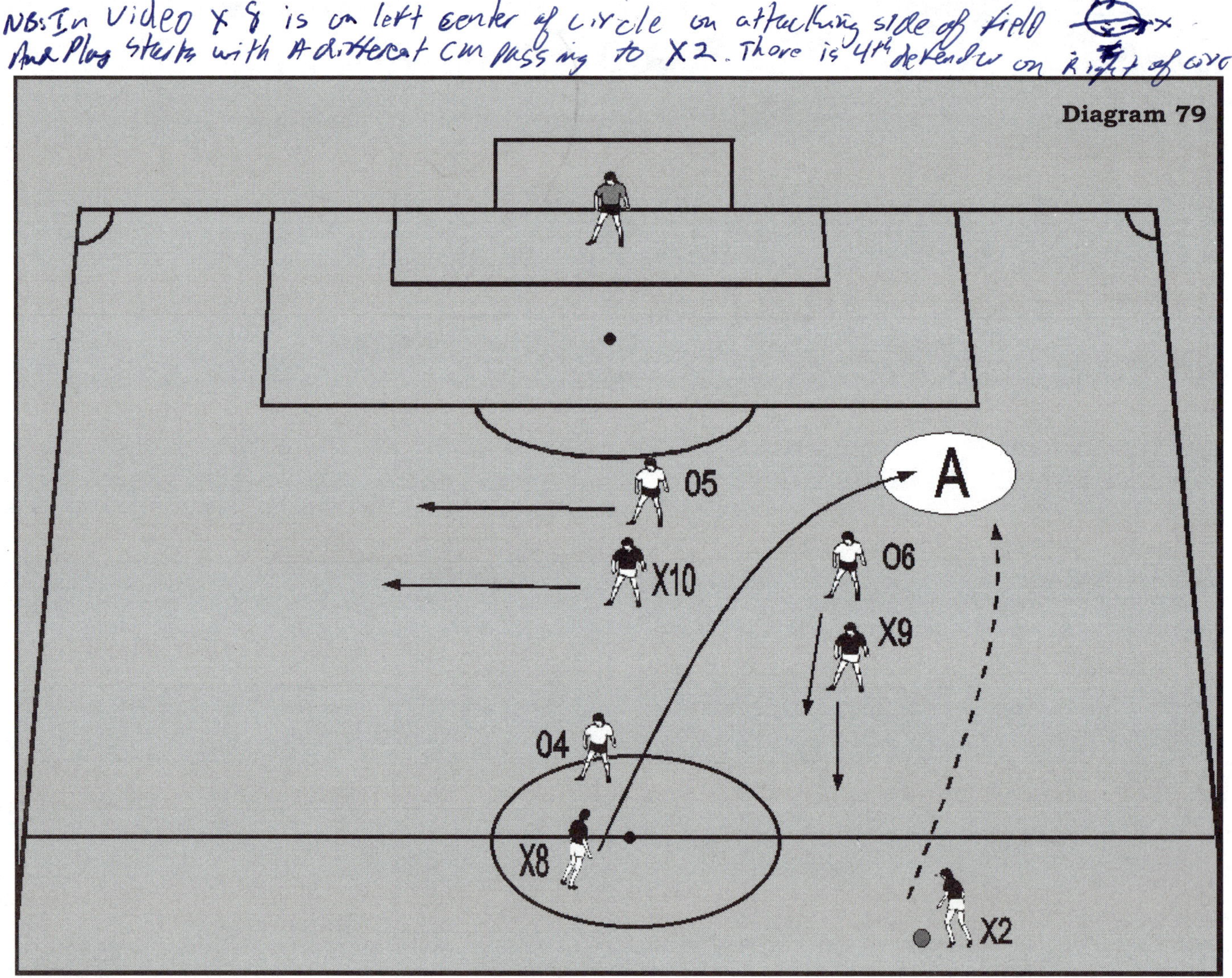

X9 comes short to show for a pass from X2 bringing his marker 06 with him.
X10 pulls away and takes his marker 05 with him.
This leaves space A that could be exploited by a run from center midfielder X8.

Obviously, if 05 and 06 don't follow the runs of X9 and X10, then the forwards would be free to receive a pass.

Having suggested some ideas of forward runs from central midfielders, a small-sided game from penalty area to penalty area is a good next step. This time organize the teams into a 2-4-2 shape. Besides being a good practice for central midfield players, this game with this shape also provides good practices for the two strikers and central defenders. The strikers can practice their movement and combinations (something we will be discussing in the next chapter) while the central defenders have to cope without a covering or spare player.

In concentrating on the central midfield players, the message that the coach needs to impart is to have them understand the circumstances when they must go ahead of the ball. First, condition all the players to stay in their position as realistically as possible. This means that the wide midfield players need to stay wide, the forwards play high up the field and so on. The central midfield players, the focus of the practice, have a little more scope but should mainly concentrate on when they should get forward. Opportunities come when a player in their team can play forward. This might be a central defender, a wide player or their midfield partner.

In the diagram below, X5 has the ball and can play forward. In this situation, X8 can make a forward run while X4 must be the holding player. Even if X5 does not play a pass for X8, the run has created space for other players.

The coach must make it clear to his players that not every run will be rewarded with a pass. Many unselfish runs must be made to improve the attacking threat.

As was mentioned earlier, the coach must make the center midfielders realize that they cannot both run forward and leave the midfield empty. However, they must avoid playing flat (side by side). In this way they are easily marked by their opponents. Ideally they play one ahead of the other, and where necessary, change places. As was shown earlier, there will be combinations to be played with the strikers and in this game the coach can highlight these movements.

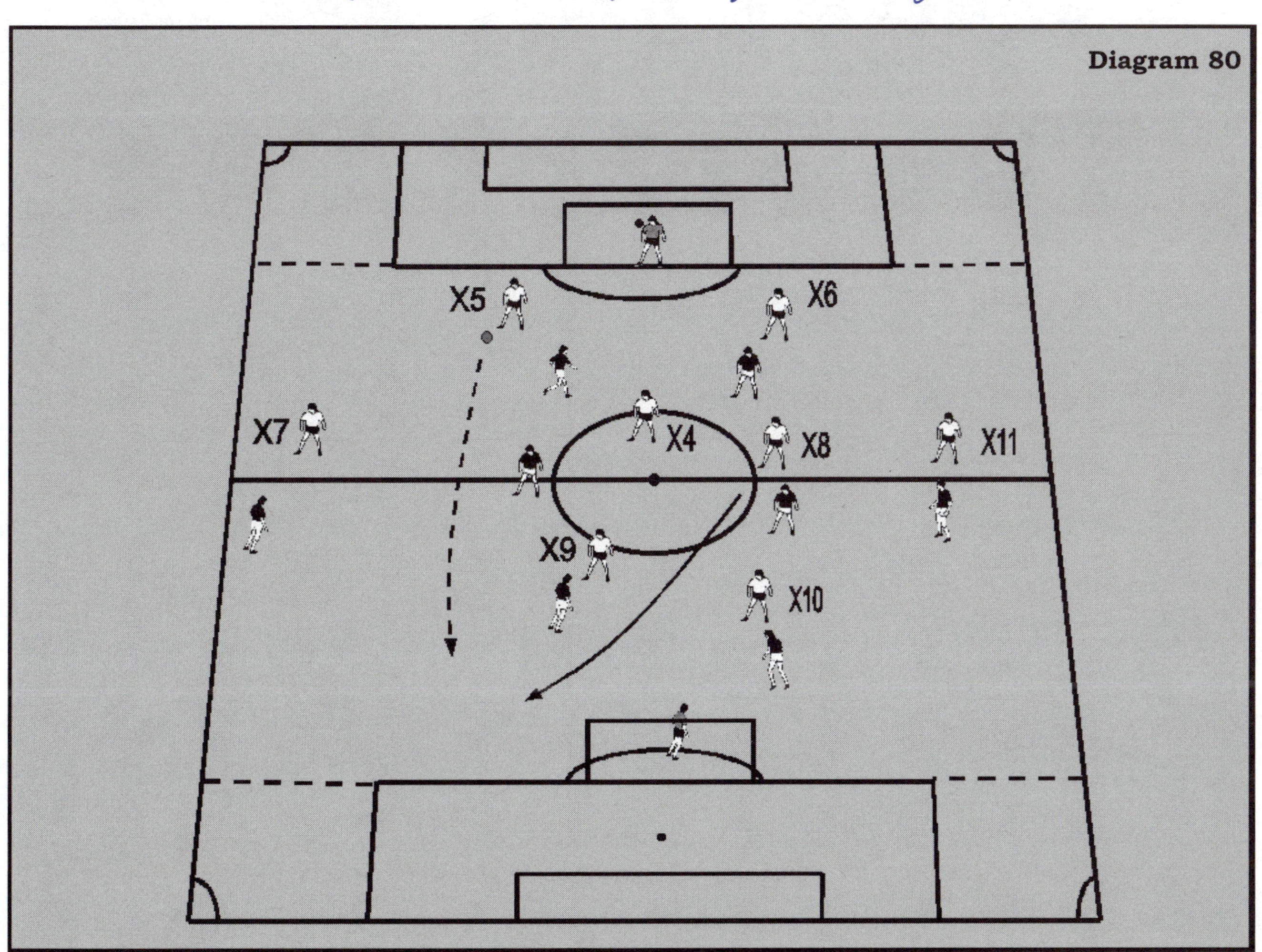

Chapter Six

Attacking With The Front Two

It is difficult to imagine a top class team not possessing at least one outstanding striker. Liverpool have Owen (England), Manchester United have Van Nistelrooy (Holland), Arsenal have Henry (France) and of course Brazil have Ronaldo. But having only one outstanding forward is to be avoided since injury to this individual can ruin the chances of success for an entire season. That's why the biggest and wealthiest clubs recruit a collection of top front men, and have usually at least three of them in their squad.

Having the fire power up front, somebody who is capable of scoring at any time in any match, is vital, and that's why vast sums of money are spent acquiring them. Of course, not every coach is lucky enough to have a Michael Owen to work with. What he can do, however, is spend time with his strikers making them as effective as possible with their movements.

The following practices illustrate some simple work that a coach can do to help improve his front players both individually and when combining together. One of the first things to have a striker appreciate is that standing still and receiving the ball is an option but not always the best option. He really needs to know how he can make life as difficult as possible for the defender marking him.

One of his 'tools' is therefore his movement. A defender must watch the ball as well as the striker and will react to the strikers movement if it poses a threat. The smart striker will use this to his advantage by making two movements to lose his marker. The first run is where he wants to take the defender, the second run is where he wants to receive the pass.

In the diagram below, X9 and X2 are in a straight line, and a straight pass makes defending easier for O5. X9 needs to be shown how to receive a pass in these circumstances and how to retain possession. But X9 must also be aware of how to improve the situation and to try to 'create' an angle for the pass this is detailed below.

All strikers start 1/2 way between penalty box and midfield line and passers start just over midfield in attacking side

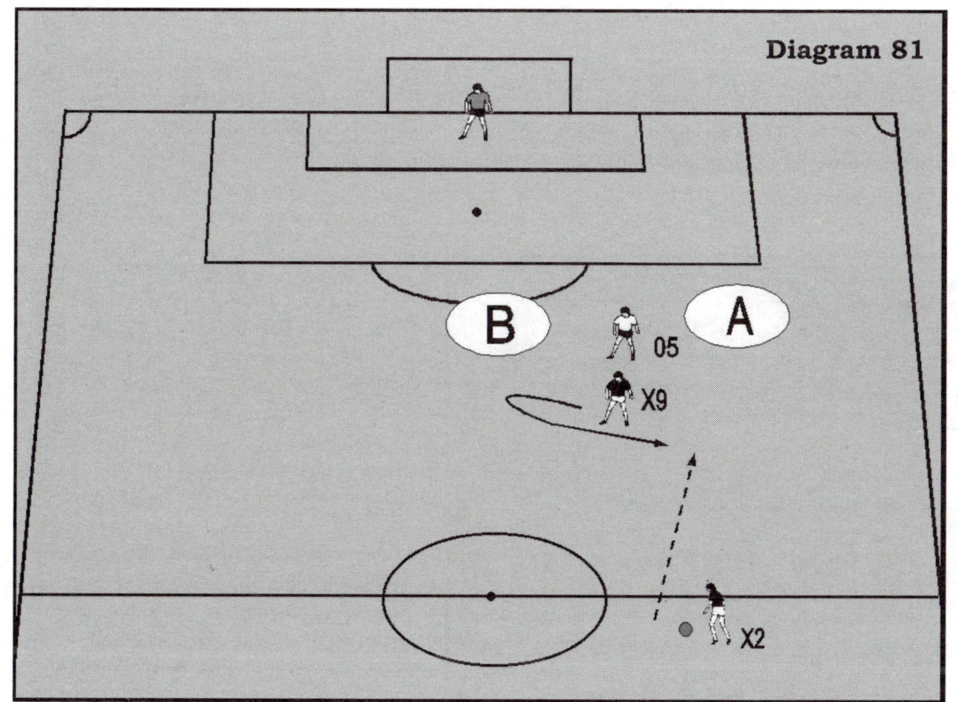

X2 touches the ball out of his feet and then passes to X9. X9 should move just as X2 is about to take that first touch. In this instance, he moves to his right first and then left, and is looking for X2 to pass the ball to space A. His intention is to move O5 by making him believe that he's going to attack space B. He then checks back to attack space A.

Although in this simple practice, X9 will not lose his marker completely, he may wrong foot him and create space for himself. With experience, a striker will sometimes make both movements very quick while at other times make the first movement slowly and then explode to lose his marker on the second run.

Also critical is the timing. If the striker does not link in with X2, then his work can be wasted. Moving too early can allow the defender to catch up, moving too late will put doubt into the mind of X2 of where to pass the ball.

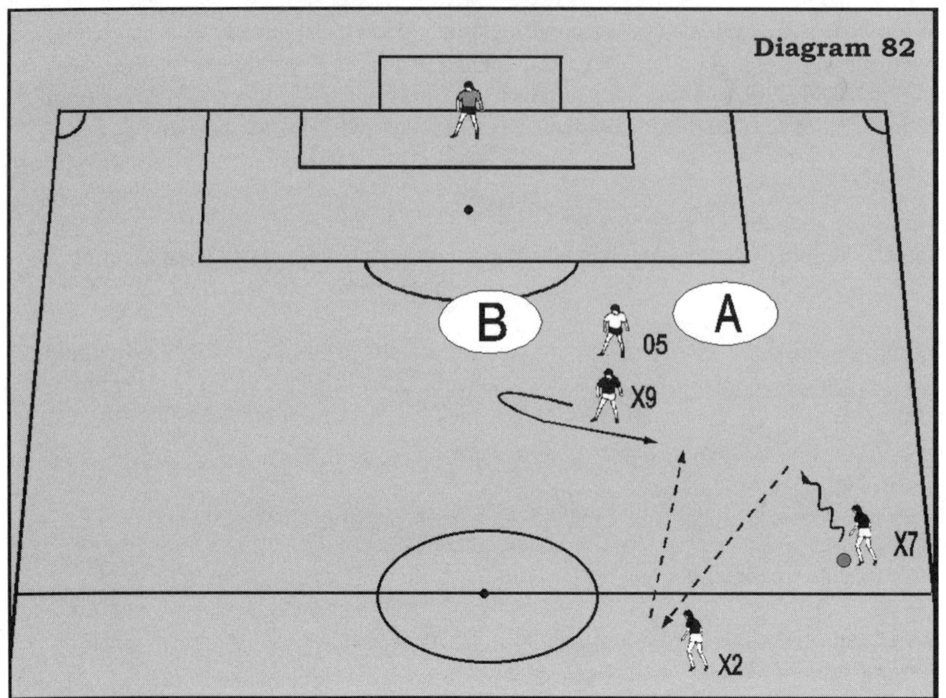

To make the timing of the runs more realistic, X7 now starts the practice by dribbling the ball 4 - 5 yards forward, turning and setting a pass back to X2. As this is happening X9 should be getting ready by doing his work - making that first run to the right - so that when the ball arrives to X2, X2 is able to play it with one touch into the path of X9's second run (to space A).

On most straight passes, X9 will find O5 marking him from behind. In the following practices X9 receives an angled pass and this gives him more options. Since is marker will now be marking the ball side, it also provides the striker with the opportunity to be 'side-on' to his marker and this is an advantage he should exploit. With the correct body position, X9 can now see his marker and this can help him to make the best decision in how to lose the defender.

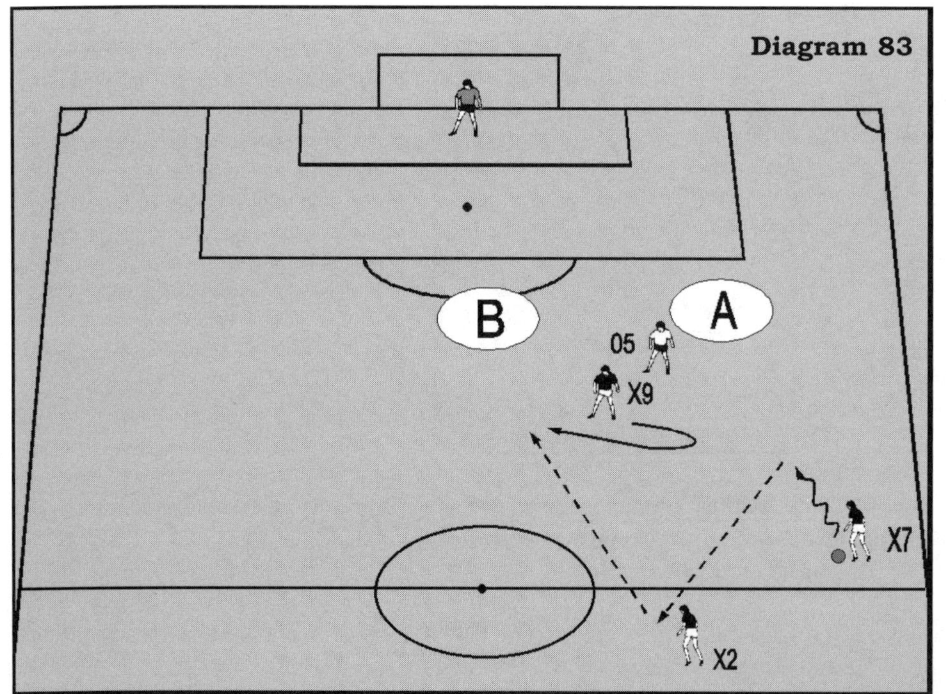

If O5 marks on his left, X9 can make the first movement in that direction and the second towards space B.

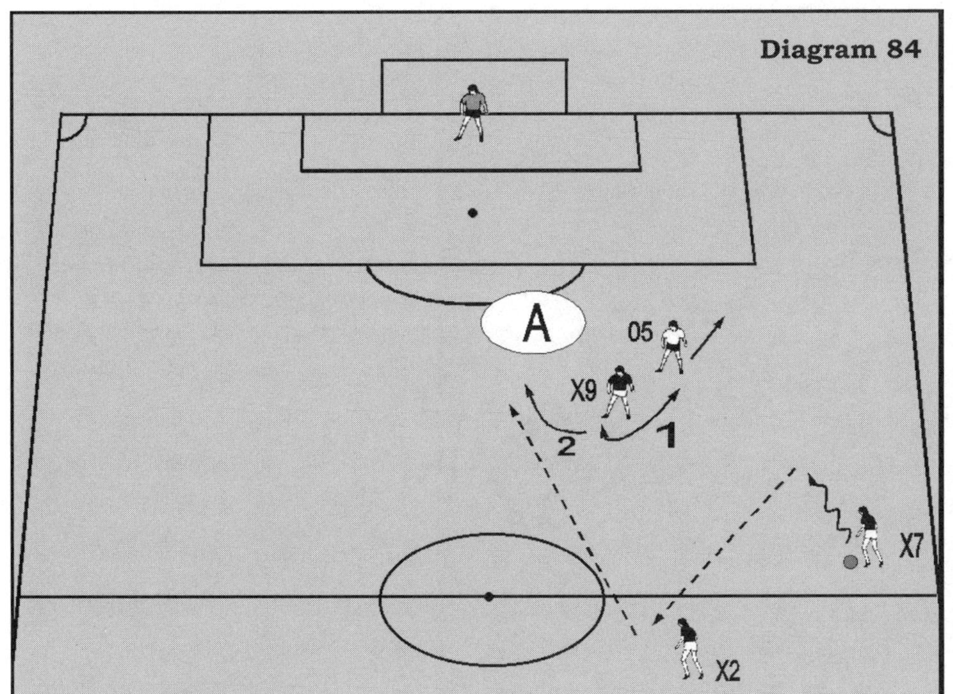

Here, X9 moves O5 back before coming across in front for a pass down the side into space A.

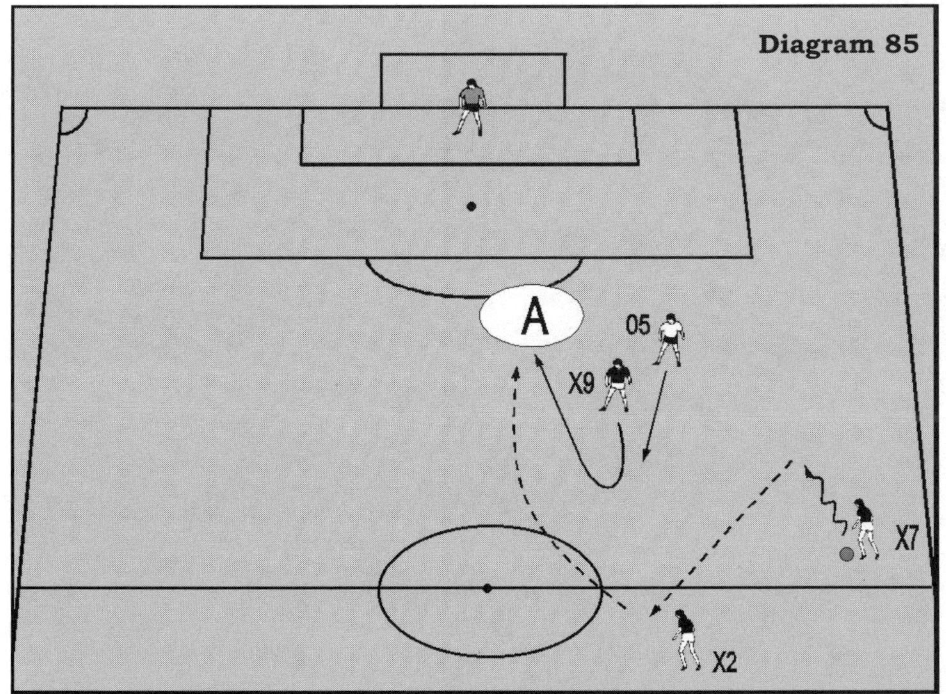

Here, X9 comes short to go long. So X2 must be ready to play the ball slightly past the striker into space A.

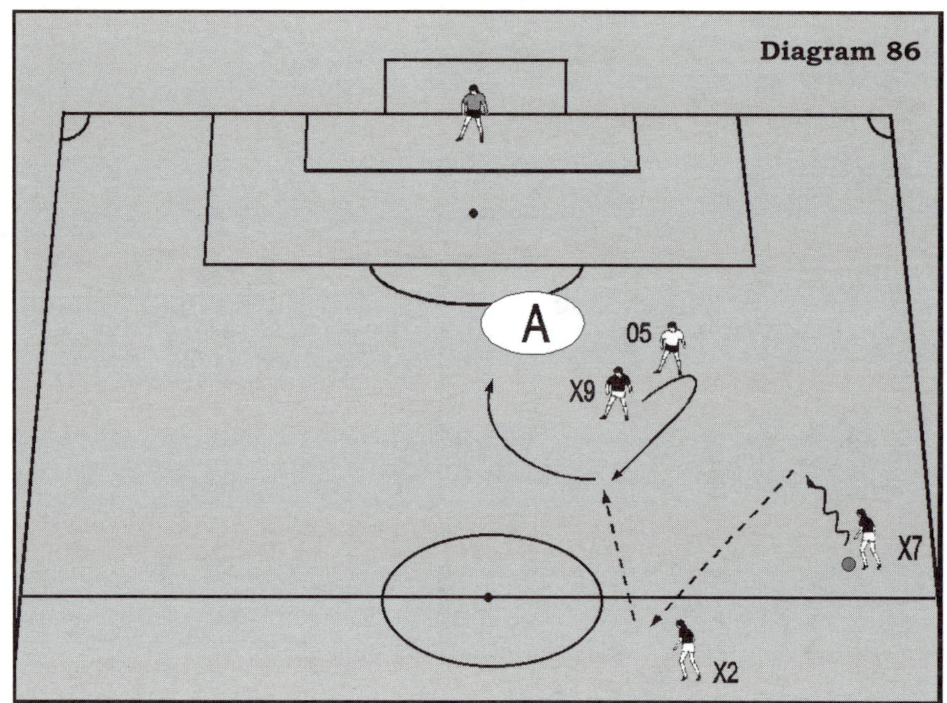

In this example, X9 goes long, checks back to receive short and then turns with the ball into space A.

The preceding practices can be performed in a 20 x 20-yard grid. Once the players understand the movements, they can be incorporated into a shooting practice around the edge of the penalty area. The striker now has the task of trying to manoeuvre himself into a shooting position. Initially the defending could be passive, but as the strikers improve, increase the tempo and have the defenders increase the difficulty.

To achieve similar results over a longer distance, consider the following two practices.

cp: one FW should move to create space for other FW, Run timing is critical, many repititions are needed to develop understanding between FWs

Diagram 87

In this practice, several players can be positioned on each of the cones. X4 plays a pass to X7 who controls and plays a longer pass (30 yards or so) on a diagonal to X9. The movement of X9 is towards X7 and then away. The coach needs to concentrate on the timing of the runs by X9 as well as the quality of pass from X7.

By having more strikers ready the practice can be repeated using X11.

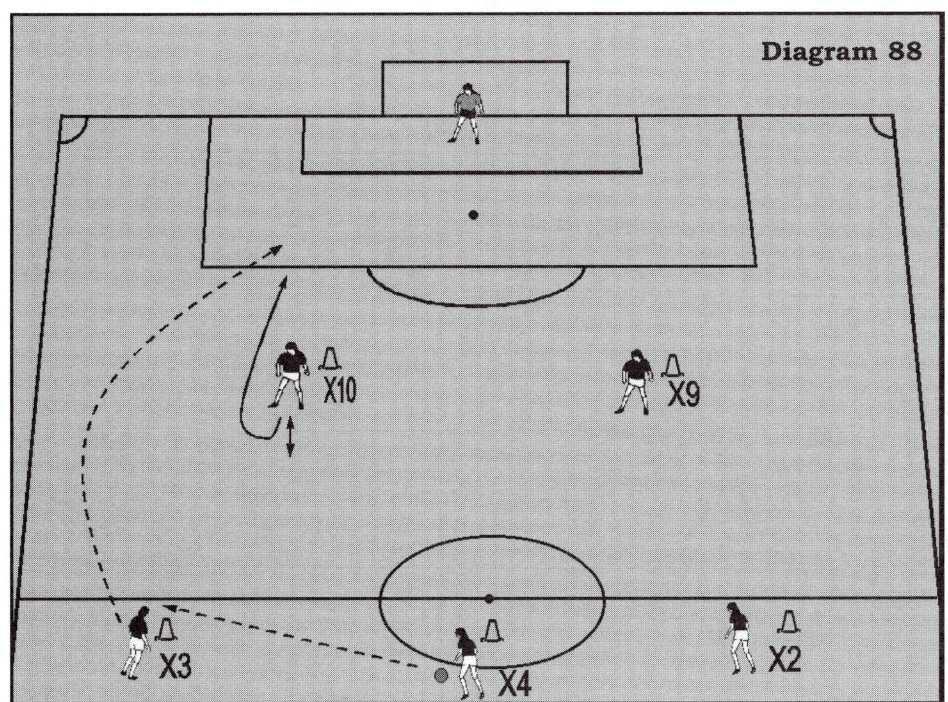

Again, several players can be involved at each station.

X4 plays to X3. This time, X10 (the striker) comes short to spin and look for a pass over the top from X3. This is a good practice, not just for the strikers and the timing of their runs, but also good technical practice for other players in the team who might have to deliver this longer type of pass.

Forward Combinations

Forwards should also learn to play as a pair, working together to create problems for defenses. The following set of practices give some suggestions of how two strikers could begin to develop an understanding of playing together by either creating space for each other or playing off each other.

All the practices can be performed in an area around the edge of the penalty area so that the moves can finish with a shot on goal and a follow-up for rebounds by the other striker.

I would recommend that much of this work is done unopposed initially, until the coach feels that the players need to be challenged. When adding defenders, start by adding one, then progress to two defenders.

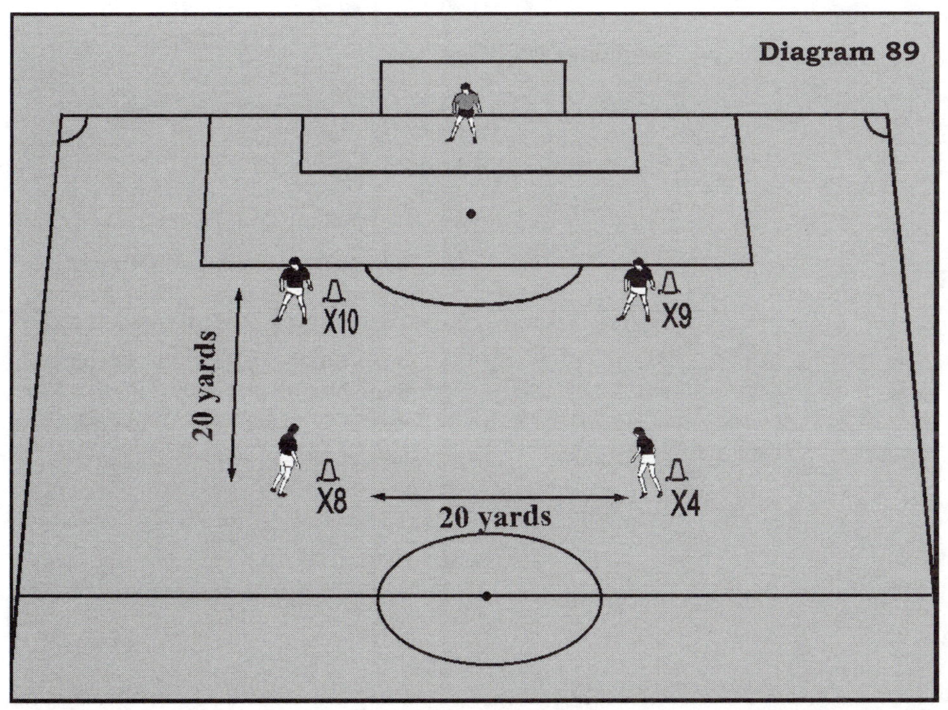

Here is the organization for practicing forward combinations. There are many permutations to these practices. These are just a few of the possibilities. For simplicity, X4 always starts by passing to X8 who then passes to the strikers.

Important points to remember when coaching these type of combinations are:-

1. X8 has to be looking to play the appropriate pass for the strikers.
2. The strikers need to work on the timing of their runs, the quality of their shots on goal and for the non shooting player to follow up.

When the coach feels the strikers are ready, he should introduce a defender to increase the challenge.

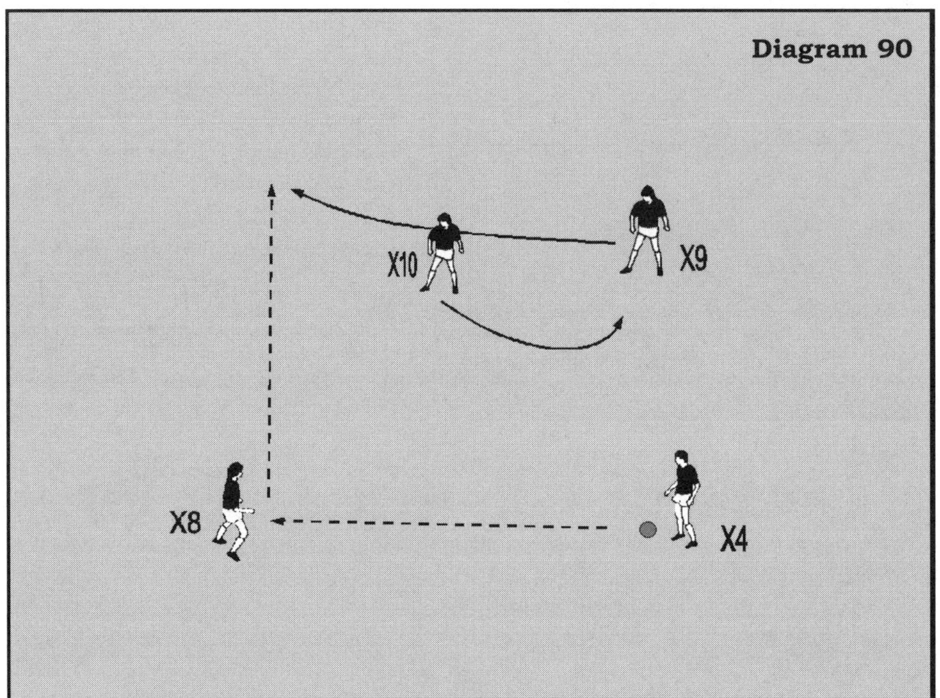

In this combination, X9 can make a run to exploit the space left by X10. Rather than run directly into the space he should consider the movements suggested in diagram 78. That is one movement away from the ball and then check back to attack the space. Having done so he should then be looking to run through and shoot on goal.

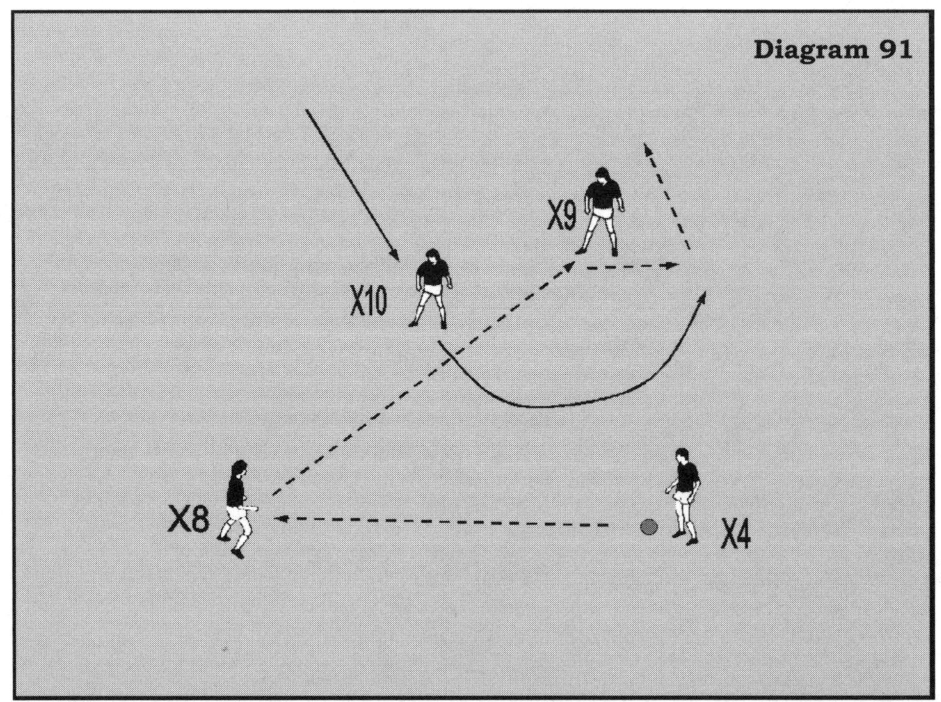

In this combination, X10 makes a diagonal run toward X4. X8 passes firmly to X9 who has held his position. X10 allows the pass to go by him and then follows. X9 sets the ball off for X10 to go on and shoot.

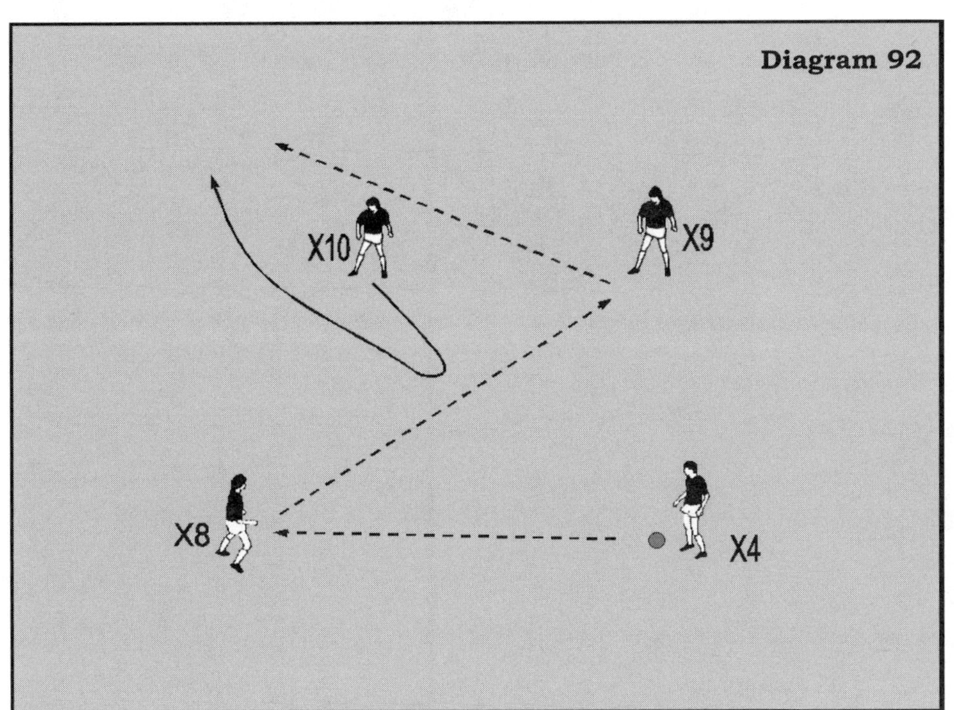

The same pass from X8 to X9. This time, X10 turns back towards his starting position to receive a pass from X9 and go on to shoot.

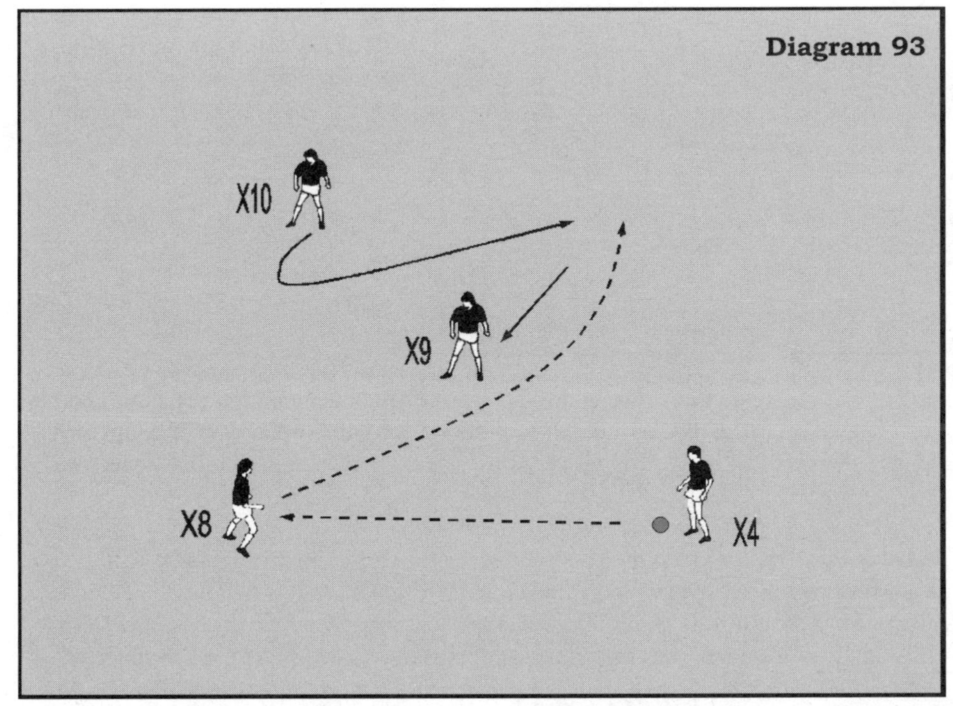

Here, X9 has now moved and come towards the ball. This obviously leaves space for X10 to exploit and go through to shoot at goal.

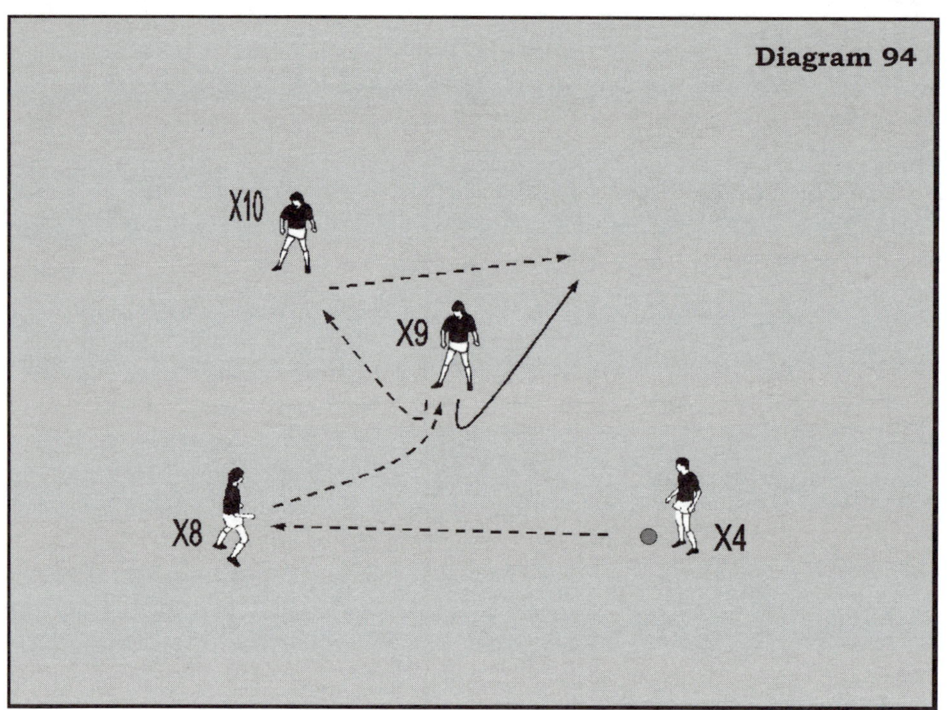

X8 plays a softer pass to X9 who plays a one-touch pass to X10 and then spins back into the space he has just left. X10 needs to be alert so that he can play a return pass into the path of X9.

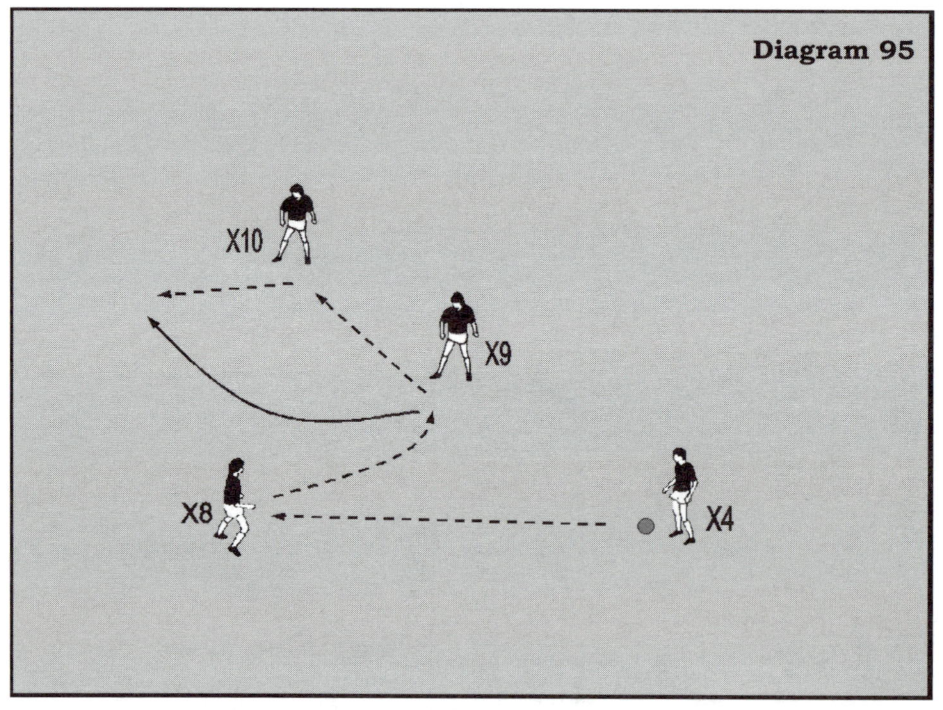

This time, when X9 receives a soft pass from X8, he plays it with one touch to X10 and then follows the ball. X10 lays it off for X9 who continues on to shoot at goal.

All of these practices take the form of drills. The real test of whether or not the players are understanding their roles comes when the coach allows them to play free. This would mean having the two strikers marked, the initial pass being played in either direction between X4 and X8, and then the two strikers getting on the same wavelength with each other - who goes short, who holds his ground and so on.

It is not unusual, given this freedom to have both strikers stand still or both move short. Only repeated practice will provide the required harmony. If this is not forthcoming, the coach may need to take a step back and remove the defenders. Having satisfied himself that the strikers are ready for a further challenge, the coach can play the small-sided game from penalty area to penalty area with a 2-4-2 formation. This will provide plenty of opportunities for the strikers to practice their individual play as well as their combinations.

Could also use 3-3-2 (only won't work for CD + CM

English Premier League Comparisons - Favorite Moves Of The Top Strikers

To complete this section on strikers, we shall look at how the three strikers mentioned at the start of the chapter, get the better of their opponents using their favorite moves.

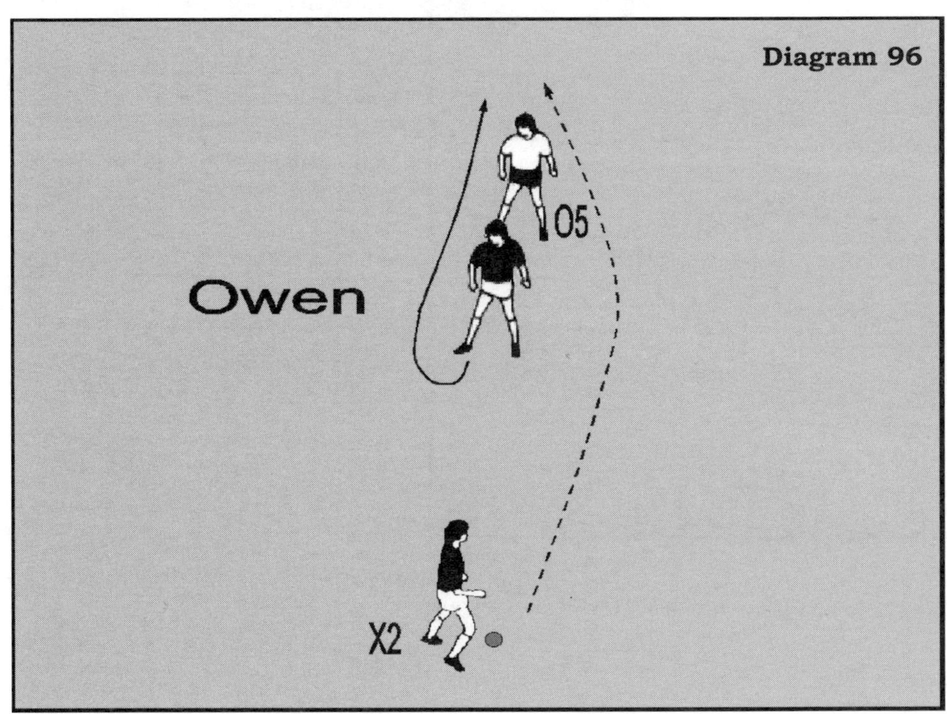

Michael Owen - Liverpool

Because of his electrifying pace, the England striker can always threaten the space behind defenders. Sometimes he needs to create that space for himself. Remember the two movements? His first movement is to bring his marker O5 towards the player in possession, X2. Because of his speed, Owen is now able to move inside, turn and sprint beyond and outside his marker. X2 has to be ready to supply the required pass.

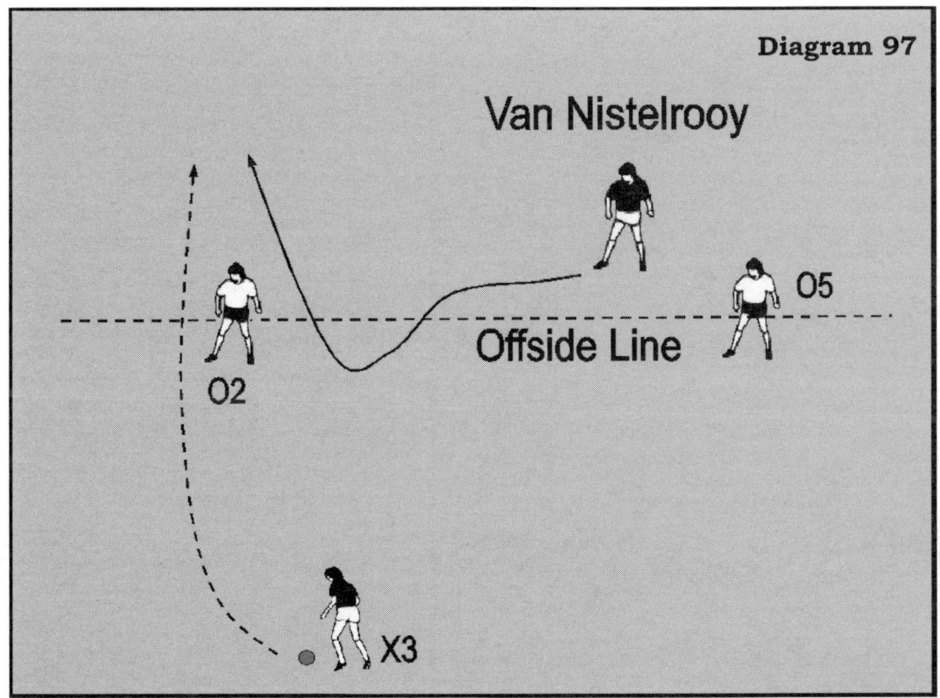

Ruud Van Nistelrooy Manchester United

The Dutchman is a master at fooling defenders. He sometimes waits in an offside position, behind defenders who lose track of him, and then with perfect timing puts himself into an onside position just before the pass is played. O5 knows that Van Nistelrooy is offside as he watches him move along the line of offside towards O2. Then as X3 looks to play his pass, Van Nistelrooy comes into an onside position. O5 very often fails to track him thinking that he will be flagged offside by the linesman.

Van Nistelrooy's run behind O2 to get on the end of the pass from X3 can therefore often be made unmarked.

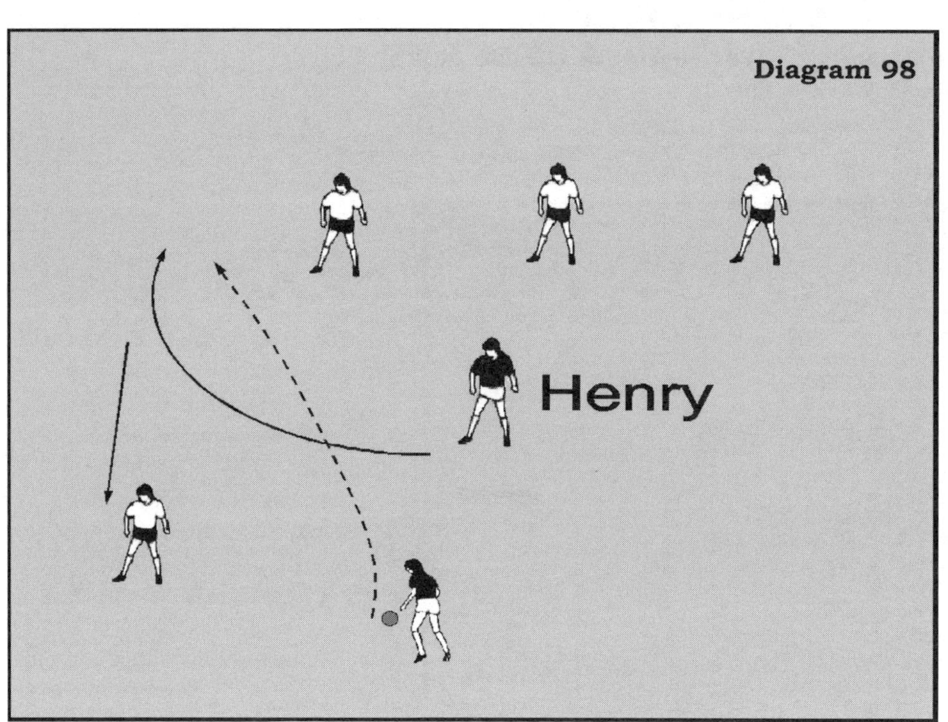

Thierry Henry - Arsenal
The French striker is at his most threatening when he exploits space on the flanks, especially the oppositions right flank.

Henry watches carefully when the opposition have possession. The moment one of their fullbacks ventures forward he looks to fill the space vacated. On a change of possession his team mates know where they can find him. If they can do this in one long pass they will.

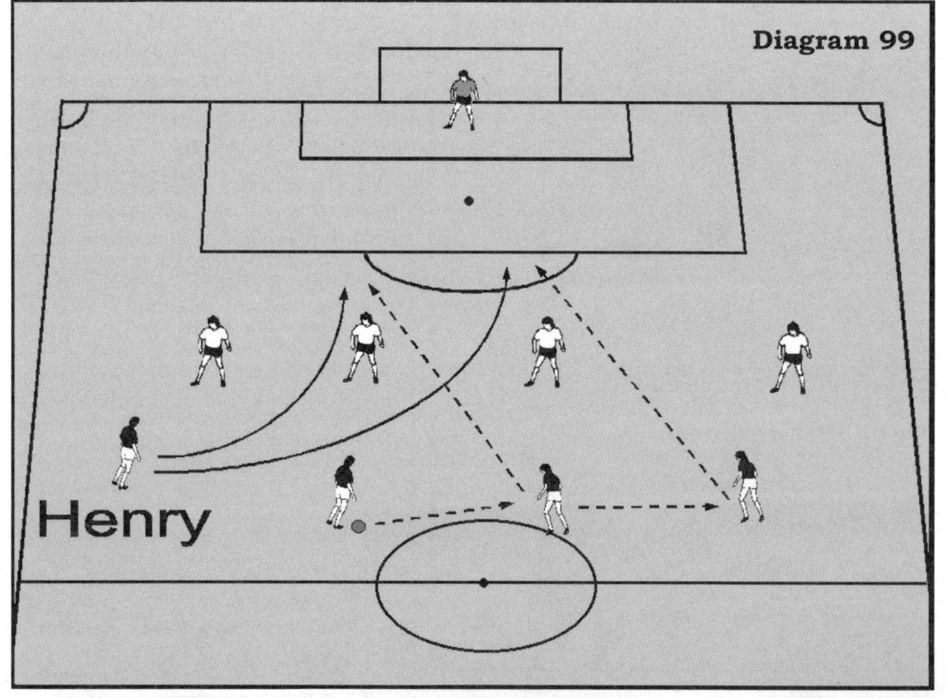

Thierry Henry - Arsenal
If he doesn't receive the ball early following a change of possession, Henry is patient enough to wait for a chance to explode inside and get on the end of a shorter pass made through the gaps between defenders. Once clear he is uncatchable.

Summary

So, having read the book, where does that leave us? For the more experienced coaches, much of what has been covered may already be familiar, although I hope that there could be one or two ideas or suggestions that will stimulate further reflection. Soccer after all is not an exact science but about opinions.

For those who are only just discovering an interest in systems of play, then the information and practices included may increase their understanding of how a 4 - 4 - 2 system can be employed. My aim in writing the book was to try and simplify the workings of the system and to outline some practices which can be used as building blocks for coaches using the 4 - 4 - 2 to organize their players.

I think it important to make the point that as far as young players are concerned, systems of play should not become a factor in their development until age 13 or 14. Younger than this they need to concentrate fully on their technical development. But for coaches working with players of an age who can understand the need to be organized then hopefully the progressive practices described will assist them in the development of their players.

References to the top English Premier League clubs, and how they utilize the 4 - 4 - 2, has been a way of explaining how every system needs to be flexible to accommodate the strengths and weaknesses of its component parts i.e. the players.

With your team you will be responsible for the emphasis you place on attack and defense. Do you want your fullbacks to overlap? Will your back four defend high or deep? Many such questions need to be addressed and the answers will come when you assess your players.

It is of course impossible to cover everything and I'm sure that some may wonder why a particular "angle" was not discussed. However, if that is the case it may just motivate you to find out more.

GOOD LUCK.

NEW BOOK

Full Season Training Program

A complete season of training sessions from Barry Gorman and the Penn State Soccer team

By Lawrence G. Fine

Only $19.95

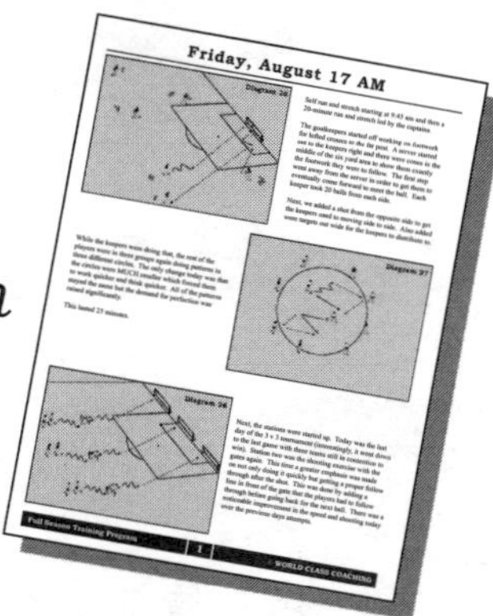

Item # 1007 - $19.95

This one-of-a-kind book by shows every training session, practice and drill of the Penn State Soccer Team from their 2001 season when they reached the NCAA Tournament round of 16.

The book starts with the two-a-day pre-season sessions, continues with the regular season training and concludes with training sessions from the post-season.

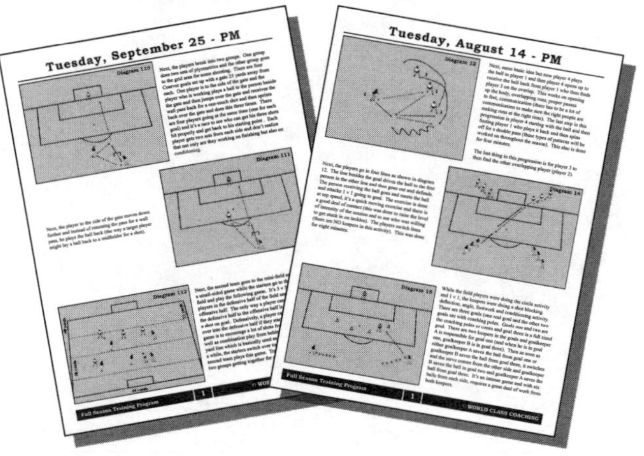

Over 80 training sessions accompanied with over 150 easy-to-read diagrams of every drill and exercise.

Coaching championship teams is a challenging and sometimes arduous task. I have known, worked with, and competed against Barry for many years, and his knowledge of the game is unsurpassed. Coach Gorman is not only a great coach, but also a gifted teacher of the game and how to coach it.

This book is a must for any serious soccer library. From start to finish you will find valuable information on how a season unfolds and how as a coach we can respond. Barry brings all of his experience and knowledge in this book and has done us all a favor by sharing it with us!

Schellas Hyndman
Head Coach, SMU Soccer

To Order Call
1-888-342-6224

WORLDCLASSCOACHING.COM

The Practices and Training Sessions of the World's Top Teams and Coaches
Edited by Mike Saif
WORLD CLASS COACHING

OR
VISIT

NOW AVAILABLE

Four new books from WORLD CLASS COACHING

These excellent books contain material from the 2000 and 2001 year issues of the WORLD CLASS COACHING magazine. Coaches of all levels will enjoy seeing what the world's top teams and coaches work on with their teams and the material in this book will be extremely helpful when planning and conducting your training sessions.

Item #1002 - $12.95

Attacking Drills of the World's Top Teams and Coaches

Includes training sessions and drills from **Manchester United, U.S. Women's World Cup Team, Venice of Serie "A", Liverpool F.C., Bodens BK of Sweden, Brazilian Youth Teams** plus many of the MLS Teams and other top teams and coaches from around the world.

Over 30 training sessions are included, each with detailed explanations accompanied with easy-to-read diagrams.

Item #1003 - $12.95

Passing and Possession Drills of the World's Top Teams and Coaches

Includes training sessions and drills from **Manchester United, Juventus F.C. and Venice of Serie "A", Ajax F.C., Lausanne of Switzerland, Liverpool Academy** plus many of the MLS Teams and other top teams and coaches from around the world.

Twenty-nine training sessions are included, each with detailed explanations accompanied with easy-to-read diagrams.

Item #1004 - $12.95

Defending and Goalkeeping Drills of the World's Top Teams and Coaches

Includes training sessions and drills from **São Paulo of Brazil, Italy U15 National Team, Tony DiCicco, Liverpool F.C., Lira Lulea BK of Sweden, Leeds United** plus **New England Revolution of the MLS** and other top teams and coaches from around the world.

Over 20 training sessions are included, each with detailed explanations accompanied with easy-to-read diagrams.

Item #1005 - $12.95

Technique and Skill Drills of the World's Top Teams and Coaches

Includes training sessions and drills from **PSV Eindhoven, U.S. Women's World Cup Team, Ajax F.C., Liverpool F.C., Leeds United, FK Teplice** plus many of the MLS Teams and other top teams and coaches from around the world.

Twenty-nine training sessions are included, each with detailed explanations accompanied with easy-to-read diagrams.

NEW BOOKS

Item # 1009 - $19.95

In ***Vision of a Champion,*** Anson Dorrance has teamed with Gloria Averbuch to create a passionate and inspiring formula for success in soccer, and in life. On fields all over the country millions dream of becoming the next Mia Hamm. This book will show them how to do it!

Anson Dorrance, the winningest women's soccer coach of all-time, gives youth players, parents and coaches the secrets of over 25 years of success developed as a collegiate (University of North Carolina) and U.S. National Team coach.

Vision of a Champion is a unique blend of technical advice and powerful inspiration. Young players, male and female, parents and coaches alike will gain enormous insight into how to develop high-level athletes, who also carry the values and lessons of competitive sports with them off the playing field.

$19.95

For Young Players

Item # 1010 - $14.95

Item # 1008 - $14.95

Soccer Coaching for 5–8 year olds

$14.95

Both books include 32 complete training sessions covering **passing; receiving; dribbling; turning; running with the ball; shooting; defending and goalkeeping**. There are also many fun small-sided games that can be used in any training session or as warm-ups. Other chapters are, Planning and Organization, The Coaching Process and Mini-Soccer Guidelines.

Clubs - Leagues - State Associations
Call for bulk discounts

These books are perfect for both the knowledgeable and inexperienced/parent coaches of young teams. The books are easy to understand and include enough training sessions to cover two complete seasons.

To Order Call
1-888-342-6224

WORLDCLASSCOACHING.COM